TAKING

— *the* —

REINS

Jimmy,
Best wishes for your
"Taking the Reins"
in your life and in
your work,

Harold Kerstedt

TAKING

— the —

REINS

Leadership, Supervision, &
Management Lessons from a Horse

HAROLD KURSTEDT
and TIM THAYNE
ILLUSTRATED BY RICH DIEHL

Published by Advantage, Charleston, South Carolina.
Member of Advantage Media Group.

ADVANTAGE is a registered trademark and the Advantage colophon is a trademark of Advantage Media Group, Inc.

Printed in the United States of America.

ISBN: 978-1-59932-344-2
LCCN: 2012949766

This publication is designed to provide accurate and authoritative information in regard to the subject matter covered. It is sold with the understanding that the publisher is not engaged in rendering legal, accounting, or other professional services. If legal advice or other expert assistance is required, the services of a competent professional person should be sought.

Advantage Media Group is proud to be a part of the Tree Neutral® program. Tree Neutral offsets the number of trees consumed in the production and printing of this book by taking proactive steps such as planting trees in direct proportion to the number of trees used to print books. To learn more about Tree Neutral, please visit **www.treeneutral.com**. To learn more about Advantage's commitment to being a responsible steward of the environment, please visit **www.advantagefamily.com/green**

Advantage Media Group is a leading publisher of business, motivation, and self-help authors. Do you have a manuscript or book idea that you would like to have considered for publication? Please visit **www.amgbook.com** or call **1.866.775.1696**

TESTIMONIALS

All too often management books can be "slow reads." Let's face it, most valid leadership concepts have been captured in previous works. So the trick becomes how to keep the reader engaged, and even entertained, so the material is understandable, believable and valuable for taking action. In *Taking the Reins*, Kurstedt and Thayne have done just that. With the clever use of horse tales and horse sense, the concepts are presented and explained in a way that will stick with me like no other work.

Mike Leinbach
Space Shuttle Launch Director

Harold Kurstedt and Tim Thayne have mastered yet another fundamental lesson of life, a story that couples the timeless interdependent relationship of horse and man, complex yet simple. The reader will recognize the power of an interactive relationship and come to better understand the significant power of trust and positive communication – horses and people excel when they "connect." Put this book on your "must read" list.

Donald J. (DJ) LaVoy
Deputy Assistant Secretary for Field Operations (PIH)
US Department of Housing and Urban Development

There is certainly no shortage of books addressing the subject of leadership. Is it helpful to have yet another one? In this case, the answer is yes! Kurstedt and Thayne have done two things better than most and have added an unusual parallel to the process of leading: the training of a horse. Within the text they attempt to answer the question, "What can the cowboy-and-horse partnership teach us about the fundamentals of leadership, supervision and management?" The answer is plenty!

The plethora of horse stories and illustrations are interesting and sometimes humorous. They are also relevant to the leadership process.

The book is well organized with one section leading logically to the next. The writing is crisp and clear. At the conclusion, one will have acquired a meaningful insight into leadership and, as a bonus, learned something about horses.

Paul E. Torgersen
President Emeritus, Virginia Tech

Kurstedt and Thayne have taken an interesting twist to management, supervision and leadership – three joined concepts that can make or break a business – in a practical, tightly written book. Starting with the premise that most of us have good intentions and positive attitudes, and sharing insights from horse training, this book is a gem of useful advice for new and seasoned managers alike.

Nancy Howell Agee
President and CEO
Carilion Clinic

Taking the Reins is a unique approach to illustrate the powerful concept of becoming a Solution-Focused leader. Harold Kurstedt's and Tim Thayne's insights on "lessons from a horse story" is not easily forgotten. It leads you to take action, apply the Solution-Focused leadership concepts, and become the leader employees want to follow. Whether new to leadership or seasoned, you'll find this book provides a lifetime of value.

Jim Heinz
Senior manager, Leadership and Organizational Development
Lockheed Martin

Regardless of where you are in your leadership journey, you can become a better leader. Kurstedt and Thayne draw beautifully on the relationship between horses and cowboys to illustrate the relationships that are possible between leaders and their staff. As you read *Taking the Reins*, you'll recognize that you may already adhere to some of their suggested principles and practices effectively. However, other suggested leadership attitudes and behaviors will unveil opportunities for growth you didn't know you had. Each chapter is a guide that will help you achieve your leadership potential to its fullest and assist you in making a bigger positive difference in your workplace.

Marta Wilson, Ph.D.
author of *Leaders in Motion* and
CEO of Transformation Systems, Inc.

Leadership is serious business. Harold Kurstedt and Tim Thayne, in their enchanting book, *Taking the Reins: Leadership, Supervision, and Management Lessons from a Horse*, beckon the reader on a surprising journey that uses the relationship between a horse and its trainer to illustrate the lessons of effective leadership. This is a delightful and generous book, for sure, but it's also unusually helpful, reframing management principles in a way that makes sense (the authors even posit pithy "horse sense" reminders throughout the book) and provides lasting food for thought and action. Thank you, Harold and Tim.

Kathy Anderson
President and CEO
Goodwin House Incorporated

I have never been a fan of leadership books until reading *Taking the Reins* by Harold Kurstedt and Tim Thayne. Leadership books typically teach the attributes necessary for leadership but do not present the appropriate methods required to implement those skills. Our industry spends significant effort in training managers to manage in ways this book teaches managers to lead. The plain speaking principles and stories resonate with the reader allowing retention of the key lessons. A must read for leaders that want to create followership.

Donald E. Stone, Jr.
PE, Chief Executive Officer, Dewberry

TABLE OF CONTENTS

DEDICATION — 19

ACKNOWLEDGEMENTS — 21

PREFACE — 25

ABOUT THE AUTHORS: MEET HAROLD KURSTEDT & TIM THAYNE — 33

PART I: WE LEAD THROUGH OTHERS' *STRENGTHS* — 39

INTRODUCTION:
ON THE MOUNTAIN, IN THE DARK — 41

CHAPTER 1:
LEADERS SURRENDER TO OTHERS' STRENGTHS — 51
*A horse will deliver the strength you need when you believe in
the horse's strength.*

CHAPTER 2:
PEOPLE NATURALLY SEEK LEADERSHIP — 59
Horses naturally seek leadership.

CHAPTER 3:
START THE RELATIONSHIP BY SPENDING
TIME LISTENING — 67
Upon first meeting a horse, a cowboy spends time listening.

CHAPTER 4:
UNDERSTANDING COMES BEFORE CONTROL – 75
Don't fight with the horse; instead, help the horse understand what you want.

CHAPTER 5:
PEOPLE'S STRENGTHS DIRECTLY REFLECT
THEIR UNIQUENESS – 83
No two horses are exactly alike.

CHAPTER 6:
A LEADER HARNESSES OTHERS' STRENGTHS – 93
A draft horse considers a harness helpful when getting ready to work.

CHAPTER 7:
WE GET WHAT WE FOCUS ON – 99
If you help your horse delight in what it can do, your horse will focus more often on what it can do.

CHAPTER 8:
ENCOURAGEMENT MAKES THE DIFFERENCE – 111
Gain the horse's trust through encouragement.

PART I: *STRENGTHS* AT A GLANCE – **119**

PART II: WE SUPERVISE THROUGH ANTICIPATING, SETTING, AND MEETING *EXPECTATIONS* – 127

INTRODUCTION:
TALMAGE AND APACHE: A DEVELOPING PARTNERSHIP – 129

CHAPTER 9:
WE ALL NEED CLEAR EXPECTATIONS AND BOUNDARIES – 145
Horses need to be given clear expectations and boundaries, and be made aware of the consequences of failing to meet those expectations or of overreaching those boundaries.

CHAPTER 10:
ALL ATTEMPTS TO MEET NEEDS OR FIX PROBLEMS RESULT IN UNINTENDED CONSEQUENCES – 155
Think two steps ahead of your horse.

CHAPTER 11:
WE RESPOND TO ENCOURAGEMENT AND REWARDS – 161
Everything you do with your horse is a form of pressure and release.

CHAPTER 12:
IN A NEW WORLD WE DO THINGS DIFFERENTLY – 171
When working with a horse, try to use a soft firmness instead of a hard tightness.

CHAPTER 13:
IT'S ABOUT CHANGE – 179
Prepare your horse to respond favorably in any set of circumstances.

CHAPTER 14:
KNOW THE PROCESS – 189
Your horse needs to be aware of each and every step of the process.

CHAPTER 15:
WHAT HAPPENED? – 197
Get your horse to look at what led to something happening.

CHAPTER 16:
WE PERFORM BEST WITH COMFORT AND CLARITY – 207
Encourage your horse to be comfortable with what's expected while you remain confident about its ability to be successful.

PART II: *EXPECTATIONS* AT A GLANCE – 217

PART II: WE SUPERVISE THROUGH ANTICIPATING, SETTING, AND MEETING *EXPECTATIONS* – 127

INTRODUCTION:
TALMAGE AND APACHE: A DEVELOPING PARTNERSHIP – 129

CHAPTER 9:
WE ALL NEED CLEAR EXPECTATIONS AND BOUNDARIES – 145
Horses need to be given clear expectations and boundaries, and be made aware of the consequences of failing to meet those expectations or of overreaching those boundaries.

CHAPTER 10:
ALL ATTEMPTS TO MEET NEEDS OR FIX PROBLEMS RESULT IN UNINTENDED CONSEQUENCES – 155
Think two steps ahead of your horse.

CHAPTER 11:
WE RESPOND TO ENCOURAGEMENT AND REWARDS – 161
Everything you do with your horse is a form of pressure and release.

CHAPTER 12:
IN A NEW WORLD WE DO THINGS DIFFERENTLY – 171
When working with a horse, try to use a soft firmness instead of a hard tightness.

CHAPTER 13:
IT'S ABOUT CHANGE – 179
Prepare your horse to respond favorably in any set of circumstances.

CHAPTER 14:
KNOW THE PROCESS – 189
Your horse needs to be aware of each and every step of the process.

CHAPTER 15:
WHAT HAPPENED? – 197
Get your horse to look at what led to something happening.

CHAPTER 16:
WE PERFORM BEST WITH COMFORT AND CLARITY – 207
Encourage your horse to be comfortable with what's expected while you remain confident about its ability to be successful.

PART II: *EXPECTATIONS* AT A GLANCE – 217

PART III: WE MANAGE THROUGH BUILDING ENDURING RELATIONSHIPS – 223

INTRODUCTION:
UNCLE JIM'S CHANGE OF HEART – 225

CHAPTER 17:
YOU CAN'T HIDE THE CONDITION OF YOUR HEART – 237
A horse will know an open heart when it sees one.

CHAPTER 18:
WE CHANGE THROUGH OUR EXCEPTIONAL MOMENTS – 247
Give a horse time to reflect on how it got somewhere, especially when it does something right.

CHAPTER 19:
THERE'S A GOOD PERSON IN THERE! – 255
Inside every horse is a good horse.

CHAPTER 20:
HELPFUL FEELINGS CONTRIBUTE TO PRODUCTIVE WORKPLACES AND HARMONIOUS RELATIONSHIPS – 263
You want your horse to make good decisions based on confidence and trust.

CHAPTER 21:
WHO ARE YOU? – 275
If you ever teach a horse a lesson in meanness, you'd better hope it doesn't learn the lesson well.

CHAPTER 22:
HUMANS ARE FRAGILE – 283
More than anything else, horses want peace.

CHAPTER 23:
YOU NEED CREATIVE, PRODUCTIVE THINKING – 293
*Get your horse to think with you. You want your horse's mind
working with you at all times.*

CHAPTER 24:
BE AWARE OF YOUR ATTITUDE'S INFLUENCE – 301
*Your horse will emulate your attitude, so choose your
attitude thoughtfully.*

FINAL THOUGHTS:
WE MUST MAKE A PLACE! – 311
*You know you've taught your horse successfully when it
demonstrates what it's learned.*

PART III: *RELATIONSHIPS* AT A GLANCE – 323

ENDNOTE – 333

AUTHOR BIOS – 337

INDEX – 341

DEDICATION

Our book is dedicated to Harold's beloved wife and Tim's very good friend, Pamela Sue Kurstedt, who "took the reins" in everything she did. As a strong leader, ground-breaking professional, confident supervisor, effective manager, caring teacher, trustworthy friend, loving wife, and compassionate mother, Pamela lived the principles presented in our book. She was, to a great many people, the world's best listener and was always other-focused. Sadly, she lost her battle with cancer and was called to be with her Lord on November 15, 2011. The hearts of many people across the US, and around the world, were deeply touched by her passing. Faithfully teaching, even to the end, Pamela expressed the following words of wisdom in a letter she wrote to her family and friends to be read at her funeral, "Why do we wait until someone is dying to tell them what they mean to us? What a difference it would make if we told our family, friends, and colleagues how they influenced us and how much we love and appreciate them. So your assignment, due today, is to tell at least one person how much they mean to you and what a difference they've made in your life." Though her spirit remains constant in our lives, her physical presence is sorely missed.

ACKNOWLEDGEMENTS

Many people supported and encouraged us in writing this book. First and foremost, our family – our wives, Pamela Kurstedt and Roxanne Thayne, and our many children – were always there to support us. We owe special thanks to Rosanne Kurstedt and Tobi Louise Kester who painstakingly worked to help the book make sense and read well. Rosanne created a comprehensive and coherent structure for our thoughts to follow. Tobi Louise brought our writing to life. They each went above and beyond the call of duty and exceeded our expectations.

Rich Diehl captured the key business-world ideas in creative, engaging horse illustrations. Rich offered solace for Harold during Pamela's diagnosis, illness and passing, when Harold needed someone to care about him.

Tim's father, Taylor Thayne, grandpa, Harry Thayne, and uncle, Jim Thayne were instrumental in bringing about the key experiences that set up each of the most significant parts of the book. These life stories not only gave us a foundation for the book chapters, but validated the concepts around which the book is organized.

We especially thank our clients, who encouraged us to capture in the book our time-tested principles upon which their workplaces and their families can change for the better.

We're indebted to the staff at Advantage Media Group who converted our manuscript into an engaging book. We thank Denis Boyles, who was immediately excited about the book content and encouraged us to pursue its publishing. Thanks to Alison Morse, who helped us launch the publishing effort, Brooke White who took the publishing project through the editing phase, Kim Hall who took the project from the design phase to completion, and to Amy Ropp, who patiently worked with us as we developed the book cover.

PREFACE

This book is about management, supervision, and leadership. Managers, supervisors, and leaders learn many principles related to their work. These are principles they must not only remember but also use as the basis for their decisions and actions. Much of the difficulty leaders have in understanding and implementing these principles stems from an inability to relate to, internalize, and transform those principles into instinctive responses to changing work situations. A collaborative relationship between a cowboy and his horse beautifully demonstrates the active use of these principles. In this book we use horse training (depicted in stories and illustrations) as the intriguing and cohesive theme around which various management, supervision, and leadership principles are effectively discussed.

Books on natural horse training are widely available. While all of them focus on training horses, some of them also include ideas that translate to improving relationships with people. Many authors of natural horse training books have been and continue to be mentors for the cowboys referred to in our book.

In *Taking the Reins*, we cite the following books on natural horse training:

- *Clinton Anderson's Lessons Well Learned* by Clinton Anderson
- *The Faraway Horses* and *Believe* by Buck Brannaman[1]
- *True Horsemanship Through Feel* by Bill Dorrance
- *True Unity: Willing Communication between Horse and Human* by Tom Dorrance
- *Cowboy Logic* and *Think Harmony with Horses* by Ray Hunt
- *Natural Horse*Man*Ship* by Pat Parelli
- *The Man Who Listens to Horses* and *Horse Sense for People* by Monty Roberts

We quote two cowboys and natural horse trainers extensively in our book: Jay Brewer of Wildcatter Ranch (just outside Graham, Texas) and Louis Wood of Mountainview Ranch (just outside

---

[1] As a natural horse trainer, Buck Brannaman, in particular, inspired Nicholas Evans's book *The Horse Whisperer* (and the subsequent movie directed by Robert Redford). Brannaman is also the subject of the Sundance documentary *Buck*.

Waynesboro, Virginia). In talking with these cowboys and watching them at work, we've gained invaluable insights into the personal relationships between man and horse, trainer and trainee. These insights validate the practicality and effectiveness of our approach to management, supervision, and leadership as discussed in this book.

Generally, the horse training industry has accepted natural horse training as a more current and effective method for training horses than other, previously used concepts. Similarly, many thought leaders in management and supervision consider Douglas McGregor's Theory Y, which assumes employees' good intentions and inherently positive attitude, as a more current and effective method for supervising people.[2] We find strong correlations between natural horse training and Theory Y. As the previous illustration demonstrates, businesspeople have a great opportunity to learn from observing and analyzing the successful implementation of natural horse training principles and practices. In other words, from a business standpoint, it's beneficial to understand the cowboy-and-horse work team or partnership. Lessons learned from natural horse training can then be applied to efforts in managing, supervising, and leading people.

The key question to be answered by this book is this: What can the cowboy-and-horse partnership teach us about the fundamentals of management, supervision, and leadership? While the horse stories and illustrations included here are intended to be interesting and memorable, this book isn't about becoming a better horse trainer. This book is about becoming a better manager, supervisor, and leader.

In the previous illustration, notice the cowboy is holding a rope and the businessman a briefcase. The point of the rope and the

---

[2] Douglas McGregor, *The Human Side of Enterprise* (McGraw Hill, 1985).

briefcase is that both are tools the cowboy and the businessman need, respectively, to help them succeed in their work. As a tool, the rope is an integral part of how most cowboys partner with their horses; ropes are used both for guiding horses and for working together (perhaps for herding and roping cattle). However, though it may appear to be a similarly integral part of business success, the businessman's briefcase may be much less useful than the cowboy's rope.

To fill your briefcase with useful, practical management tools, we have organized this book around the three essential components of effective management, supervision, and leadership:

- strengths, discussed in Part I;
- expectations, discussed in Part II; and
- relationships, discussed in Part III.

To introduce each component, we pull applicable lessons from a horse story. After each story, we include a brief introductory section that describes the lessons we discuss in subsequent chapters about that component. Sprinkled throughout the text are little boxes of "horse sense," or key insights in nugget-sized form. We believe this organization will enable you to connect each lesson to ideas about management, supervision, and leadership, while also allowing you to develop your comprehension of these concepts more fully. This book is organized in a way that allows you to dip in and out, so you can gain the information most applicable to your needs at any given time.

In writing this book, we intended to provide you with easy-to-remember ideas about and examples of management, supervision, and leadership that you can effectively implement in your everyday work. Just as a horse and rope are integral parts of a cowboy's success, we want the insights in this book to become integral tools you use to complete tasks successfully as you work with subordinates and supervisors alike.

Since this book is about management, supervision, and leadership, we should carefully consider how we define each of these terms. These three words are not interchangeable; they have different meanings. In the workplace, we play many different roles, and we make decisions specific to each of those roles.

- MANAGEMENT:
  For the purpose of this book, management is decision making: nothing more, nothing less.

- SUPERVISION:
  Supervisors make decisions (manage) about resources, most notably financial and human resources. Most people use the word *manager* where we would use the word *supervisor*.

- LEADERSHIP:
  Leaders recognize the strengths of those around them. They affirm, encourage, gather, and move these strengths toward a mutually-accepted vision. Leaders make decisions (manage) related to identifying problems, determining and achieving visions, and developing organizational culture.

Any one manager, supervisor, or leader may also be assigned to or take on many additional roles, such as those of a facilitator, coach, and follower. In each case, the person makes decisions reflecting the role's responsibilities.

In *Taking the Reins*, we discuss the concept of solution-focused leadership at length, emphasizing the fact that this type of leadership focuses on strengths. If our focus is on fixing weaknesses, damage control is typically the result; in contrast, if our focus is on improving strengths, excellence is the more likely result. We choose to strive for excellence.

There are two basic management and supervision theories: Theory X, which is negative in assumptions, relies on threats and coercion. It is analogous to older practices of horse training (taking weeks to "break" the horse). Theory Y, which, as we discussed earlier, is positive in its assumptions, is predicated on shared goals. It is analogous to natural horse training (training the horse relatively quickly, sometimes in a matter of minutes). Our descriptions and discussions of supervision in this book rest on the tenets of Theory Y, which often parallel tenets of natural horse training.

The working relationship between a cowboy and a horse on a ranch parallels the working relationship between a leader or supervisor and worker or staff member in the workplace. In each case, the relationship's two participants want to be a part of, and contribute favorably to, an effective, productive team. If you've been immersed in a Theory X environment for a long time, such a connection may seem like a stretch. However, by the end of Chapter 1, we believe you'll be looking at your role as leader or supervisor very differently than you did when you first picked up this book. You might even picture yourself in a snappy western shirt and cowboy hat, entering the cubicle-corrals to establish relationships of trust and partnership with your team. So, cowboy-up, pardner, and let's *mooo*-ve on.

ABOUT THE AUTHORS

MEET HAROLD KURSTEDT
AND TIM THAYNE

The partnership of Harold Kurstedt and Tim Thayne sparked an interest in writing about leadership based on the surprising perspective of lessons learned from a horse. This partnership, though, may seem to be an unlikely pairing of their skill sets.

Harold Kurstedt is an engineer who also teaches management, supervision, and leadership classes at Virginia Tech. He facilitates workshops on these topics for working professionals.

Tim Thayne is a marriage and family therapist who runs a business focused on helping teens with emotional or drug-related issues through developing healthy, productive family environments.

What Harold and Tim have in common is an understanding of horses, and what you can learn from spending time with the animals. Harold and Tim both have ranch or farm backgrounds. Tim was raised on a horse ranch in Utah. He spent a good portion of his youth horseback riding, along with milking cows, tending sheep, watching wildlife, and working alongside his dad in excavation construction. Tim still works with horses both at his home and on the family ranch. For many years, Harold lived with his family on a 300-acre farm in the Appalachian Mountains. The farm included horses, cows, and plenty of outdoor activities for his six children.

Together, Harold and Tim have developed a relationship-oriented solution-focused leadership program, which they frequently present to business and government organizations. In their professional lives, they have realized that reaching the highest levels of success (in both management and family therapy) often depends on building trusting relationships among different people with different priorities. This realization has carried over into the development of trusting relationships in their personal lives. Only when trusting relationships are developed, Harold and Tim believe, can one expect to become a truly successful manager, supervisor, and leader.

Though their friendship and working relationship began just eighteen years prior to this book's publication, in their own ways both Harold and Tim have been working toward developing the content for this book for decades. When a mutual friend introduced them, Tim and Harold found themselves energized. They shared beliefs about the skills, knowledge, and practices needed by people at mid-to-upper levels of supervision to achieve project goals while fostering employee growth. These same values support long-term success within an organization.

At the time of their first meeting, Harold had two primary responsibilities in his capacity as professor and administrator. First, he coordinated Virginia Tech's activities in outreach and continuing education for practicing professionals. Second, he taught management systems engineering to scores of undergraduate and graduate students.

Tim, also immersed in academia, was a doctoral student at Virginia Tech, where he was working on a dissertation for his degree in marriage and family therapy (MFT) and teaching family relations classes. Tim had struggled with whether to focus on organizational behavior or on MFT, both of which interested him greatly. Unwilling

to choose one over the other, he eventually blended his two interests in a dissertation project that incorporated marriage and family therapy techniques into his own approach to developing workplace leaders.

After recognizing their similar perspectives, Harold and Tim joined forces to design and develop an outreach program titled Solution-Focused Leadership. The program included two intense, three-day experiential training sessions separated by a three-month coaching period. The coaching period offered participants support for the changes in attitude and behavior to which they had committed during the initial training session.

Tim and Harold developed their Solution-Focused Leadership program in 1996 and within a few years had delivered the program to more than twenty-five groups (each group included twenty people) in business and government organizations. The program continues to be a favorite in whole or in part with businesses, government organizations, and professional associations in the United States and abroad. The program's underlying premise almost amounted to a classic mission statement: "A Solution-focused leader recognizes the strengths of those around him or her, affirms and encourages the further development of those strengths, harnesses those strengths, and guides the team toward a mutually agreed-upon vision."

Participants of the hugely successful program, including super-visors and organizational leaders, continually commented that it had offered the most useful training they had ever received. Many frequently said they were "blown away" by the fact that their company had funded their participation in the program. Attendees also reported experiencing unanticipated success at home as they applied the course's principles to family interactions and implemented their new skills throughout their personal lives.

After working on the Solution-Focused Leadership program, Harold and his wife, Pamela (also an engineer, professor, and administrator at Virginia Tech), moved their family to the Washington, DC area. Together, the couple formed Newport Group, LLC, through which they continued to train, consult, and educate industrial and government clients nationwide. Harold and Pam discovered the foundational concepts of the Solution-Focused Leadership program were at the heart of many services and products they delivered to their clients. Eventually, working well past when they had expected to retire, and wanting to be close to family again, Harold and Pam picked up once more and settled back in the Appalachian Mountains.

Meanwhile, after his graduation, Tim and his wife, Roxanne, returned home to their extended family in Utah. Tim continued using the Solution-Focused Leadership program training at his new company, Thayne and Associates. He cofounded Outback, a wilderness-based treatment program for teens with emotional or drug-related problems. Through his work at Outback, Tim noticed a dangerous gap in the treatment of these teens when they returned home. He recognized only a superhuman individual would be able to maintain the changes made during the wilderness treatment period once the teen returned to a familiar environment with familiar problems, the very problems that might have caused him or her difficulty in the first place.

Applying previous research to a creative process, Tim and Roxanne founded Homeward Bound, an aftercare program that helps parents consciously and thoughtfully prepare their home environment in ways that will support their child's continued progress after treatment, providing the opportunity for better long-term outcomes. Today, this nationwide program, which uses many of the Solution-Focused Leadership program's concepts and principles, works in the homes of hundreds of families. Success in and desire for continued growth of this effort has resulted in the development of curricula, online tools, and products focusing on family leadership and communication.

Today, Tim and Roxanne have carved out a little farm in the middle of the city in Lehigh, Utah, where they continue their work with Homeward Bound.

Over the last several years, Harold and Tim have happily reestablished their professional work relationship. Through reminiscing and sharing their accomplishments since they first developed and implemented the Solution-Focused Leadership program, the two found their similar perspectives on life energizing them once again. Ultimately, that energy resulted in the collaborative spirit necessary for writing this book. In talking about their varied passions, Harold and Tim recognized the significant and valuable parallels between working effectively with a horse as a cowboy-horse team and managing, supervising, and leading people effectively in the workplace. For the authors, it seemed only natural to definitively establish a theory of behavior based on their first-hand experiences with magnificent horses and their well-developed understanding of business organization and leadership.

The cowboy and his horse form an important partnership that accomplishes assigned tasks and achieves results. Each brings very different strengths to the partnership, but for that partnership to succeed, both parties must have similar goals. Harold and Tim make a great team; they have very different strengths but very similar worldviews.

PART I

WE LEAD THROUGH OTHERS' *STRENGTHS*

INTRODUCTION

ON THE MOUNTAIN,
IN THE DARK

TIM THAYNE: My family and I enjoyed riding our horses into the High Uintah Mountains of northeastern Utah, spending time together, finding solace in nature, and fishing in the mountain streams and lakes. I remember one trip in particular. It was when my grandpa asked me if I would like to fish in a high mountain lake he remembered from his youth. Even though the lake was hours away, and far from any trail, I could sense his eagerness to find the old fishing spot. Many years ago, as a boy of twelve or thirteen, while herding sheep in the mountains during the summers, Grandpa had fished there with his father. Yet he hadn't been there since.

So, with an adventurous spirit, my grandpa, my brother Tracey, and I left the rest of the family at camp and headed up the trail with our horses. The trail quickly led us out along the dizzying edge of a steep cliff. We found ourselves above a dark canyon, where we could hear a rushing river far below.

We followed the trail for half an hour. Then, at Grandpa's direction, we turned off the trail for another hour. In the bright daylight, I could see we had already made it high above the timber-line, where trees didn't have enough oxygen to grow. Almost casually, Grandpa pointed out a peak in the distance and said, "There should be a lake at the base of that mountain. That's where we're going."

Our small posse turned again, moving swiftly northward through a high mountain valley, strewn with large boulders, with Grandpa's ever-watchful eye focused on the peak. At last, we were greeted by a little snowpack that fed into a small lake. We had arrived. I marveled at the incredibly vivid, pristine beauty of the world around me.

Before I could get my horse tied up and my fishing pole rigged, Grandpa was shouting, "I got one!" Suddenly, my hands were shaking with excitement, and I couldn't get my fly tied on fast enough. Before I could make it to the water's edge with reel in hand, Grandpa had landed his second fish.

Much to our utter surprise and complete joy, nearly every cast produced a small trout. We were indeed far off the usual trail, in a place where few visitors ventured, and those unsuspecting trout were hungry. We each found our own spot along the shore and settled in. Our collective excitement was palpable. We couldn't help but spur each other on in the fun, yelling across the lake to one another and having the time of our lives.

Before we knew it, the sun was going down and clouds had moved in. The wind whipped around us with a howl. Looking up, I could see an ominous storm brewing. Suddenly, night fell and, unfortunately for us, clouds mostly obscured the moon. It was pitch dark. The nightfall had come so fast that we were caught completely unprepared. We had no flashlights, no matches, and nothing to warm us or light the way.

I stood for a moment, stunned and very afraid. My mind raced with seemingly unanswerable questions. How could we survive the night without shelter? None of us had even a jacket. What would we eat? How would we protect ourselves? What was out there in that darkness? It didn't occur to me to try to make the treacherous journey back to camp. However, that's exactly what Grandpa told us we were going to do.

With complete authority and presence of mind, Grandpa said calmly, "Guys, let's get on our horses. I'll take the lead. Just tie the reins together, so they don't fall; then, we'll lie down in the saddles, put our arms around the horses' necks, and let them go. They'll take us back to camp."

I didn't believe what my grandpa said. Anxiously, I told him, "I can't see my hand in front of my face now." The only senses I had left were touch, smell, and hearing, and my intense fear clouded each of those. I was fighting against a fear that threatened to consume me. More questions streamed through my mind. Even if we made it back to the main trail, back to the place where we had turned off to get to the lake, how could the horses see well enough to go around the cliffs? If we couldn't control the horses, how could they possibly *not* misstep, thereby throwing us into the canyon and river below? How could any of us hang on for that long? What if we got separated somehow?

On top of everything came my greatest, longtime fear: a fear of heights. To this day, I remain afraid of heights. However, I also knew that if I started to act frightened, the fear would become contagious and the horses would also become frightened.

In the end, there was no question in Grandpa's mind; there was no changing the plan. All I could do was to get into my saddle, hold on for dear life, and ride it out.

Except for our low, encouraging, and reassuring murmurs to the horses, in whom we each placed our full trust, the three of us said very little for the next hour and a half as we clung to our saddles and horses, staying low to keep from being brushed by the trees off the animals' backs. At a steady pace, in single file, the horses carried us forward through the dark. They seemed to know where they were going.

When I began to hear the river getting closer, I knew we were returning to the main trail. Being on the main trail brought me both a sense of hope – it seemed miraculous we had made it that far – and, simultaneously, heightened anxiety. I feared the stretch ahead, a mere hundred yards or so, at most. One small slip or stumble and we could plunge into the darkness below. I tightened my grip on the saddle horn with one hand and my embrace of my horse's neck with the other.

In time, the sound of the river faded, and I knew we had safely passed the terrifying cliff. In that moment, as my racing heart slowed to a more normal rate, I finally understood our only hope had been in using the horses' innate strengths – strengths we humans didn't possess – effectively.

Eventually, as we kept moving, we started to see flickers of light. Our campfire could be glimpsed behind the trees. For the first time since climbing into the saddle on our return journey, I took a deep breath, relaxing completely. As I realized we were safe, a feeling of intense gratitude for my horse swept over me.

To this day, I still marvel at how the horses brought us safely to camp that dark night. When we had begun our trek down the mountain, I hadn't known where the undirected horses would take us. We could have ended up in Wyoming or we could have ended up dead. Yet, given our complete trust and willingness to place our lives on their backs, these magnificent animals protected and transported us to our desired destination. I had had no idea how to get there or how to plan the journey. However, as it turned out, my grandfather had been through that before. Much like the horses, Grandpa, in whom I had also placed my faith and trust, was a vital resource in this desperate time of need.

Later, I thought about how vast and unsettled the wilderness had seemed and how small a dot on a map our campfire was. The horses' natural homing sense, keen ability to see in the dark, and surefootedness gave us the ability to reach our goal. Because of the horses, we didn't have to spend a freezing night huddled together, trying to survive.

Tim's story about a crisis in the dark in the mountains has many lessons, which we'll discuss in the chapters noted in parentheses:

1. *The leader took control.* Who was the leader in this story? Grandpa. Grandpa knew the horses had strengths and would deliver when he, Tracey, and Tim surrendered control. Leadership didn't come from being in front; instead, leadership came from having the wisdom to release control at the right time, in the right place, and to the right individuals (Chapter 1).

2. *Decisive leadership works.* Grandpa's reassuring authority over and command of the situation allowed Tim and Tracey to understand and accept his vision as their own. Grandpa accurately assessed the situation quickly and effectively. As a result, he was able to help himself, his grandsons, and their horses arrive at a mutual vision: getting back to safety as efficiently as possible. The horses may have wanted to get back to the other horses, while Tim, his brother, and his grandpa wanted to get back to their family members, but that difference doesn't matter. The motivations may have been different, but the vision was the same (Chapter 2).

3. *Knowing when to trust others can lead to an unexpected triumph.* Tim had to have trust and take a leap of faith. Sometimes, supervisors need to let go of desires to maintain control by trusting others, taking leaps of faith, and seeing what's possible when they let go. And what are trust and faith, in these contexts? Trust is yielding to others' strengths when we know strengths are present. To do otherwise is to invite failure. Grandpa trusted the horses' strengths because

he knew horses. As this story teaches us, faith is what time requires. Having faith means yielding to strengths we don't even know are there. Tim had to believe his grandpa knew not only what strengths the horses had but also how to harness those strengths and have faith the horses would save them (Chapter 2).

4. *Understand all the resources available to you.* Grandpa knew the horses well, so he was confident in their ability to get their riders home safely. What's more, Grandpa also knew Tim and Tracey. He knew they would follow him when asked, and he gave them effective and reassuring guidance (Chapter 3).

5. *Knowing which individuals can be trusted is essential.* Leadership isn't participating in frivolous surrender; instead, it includes occasional surrenders based on knowing what considerations to incorporate into your decision making. A wise leader understands the instincts, perceptions, and skill sets of those people to whom he or she releases control, and, often, a wise leader gives those people (or horses, in Tim's case) the benefit of the doubt. In short, when Grandpa decided his party should release control to the horses, he knew what he was doing (Chapter 3).

6. *You don't need an emergency to become a wise leader.* Not all decisions to release control and surrender to others' strengths occur in crisis situations. When you're not in a crisis, you have to decide how, when, and to whom you should release control during a crisis. Trust those closest to the envi-

ronment in which the work must be done. They're likely to understand specific, pertinent details and will be able to apply skills they've developed in response to experiencing that particular environment frequently. In Tim's story, the horse is closer to nature, where the problem lies. In the workplace, the worker is closer to the work (Chapter 4).

7. *Let others' talents shine.* Based on the horses' training and connection to their riders, Grandpa knew if he gave them the opportunity, the horses would display their unique and needed strengths. The horses would want to use their strengths to the best of their abilities, perhaps changing from following the rider's direction to giving the rider direction (Chapter 5).

8. *Know how to win.* Having the right systems and procedures in place allows people to recognize and exercise strengths required for success. By telling Tim to release the reins and lie low in the saddle, Grandpa was also encouraging the horse to concentrate on the task at hand and use its homing strength to get home. Grandpa's encouragement gave the horses all the support needed for them to complete their task successfully (Chapter 5).

9. *We get what we focus on.* In this crisis, what did Grandpa focus on? He focused on the instinctive strengths of the horses. As a result, the horses brought their instincts to bear on the problem. Next, what did the horses focus on? The horses focused on their herd instinct, which was to get back to the other horses in camp. As a result, the horses did what

was needed: they headed home. Finally, what did Tim focus on? He focused on his trust in his grandpa. Tim's grandpa, in turn, knew he could trust the horses. As a result, Grandpa's knowledge and experience fit what was needed and thereby resolved the situation (Chapter 7).

10. *Have faith.* By being calm and confident in a difficult situation, Grandpa encouraged his grandsons to trust in the strengths of the horses. Tim and his grandpa demonstrated trust as they encouraged the horses down the steep mountain by calmly caressing the horses' necks, encouraging them, and staying low. A sense of security, strength, and confidence resulted in both the people and the horses (Chapter 8).

In Your Workplace ...

The principles and practices illustrated through this story about Tim and his grandpa give us an engaging entrée to Part I ("We Lead through Others' *Strengths*"). In this section, we discuss the relationship between leadership, strengths, and vision. Strengths and vision are two significant components of the Solution-Focused Leadership program. We have organized this section's chapters by a progressive process of thought:

- You build your leadership on others' strengths (Chapter 1).
- You understand the situation at hand and can formulate a vision mutually recognized and accepted by everyone on your team (Chapter 2).
- You understand your people and their unique strengths because of your listening skills; this understanding allows

you to gather team abilities needed to achieve the vision (Chapter 3).

- You help your people know you and what you need from them to achieve the vision (Chapter 4).
- You help everyone better understand the work team's collective strengths (Chapter 5).
- You give support for recognizing and harnessing team strengths, propelling the team to achieve the vision (Chapter 6).
- You get what you focus on, so focus on strengths and vision to ensure you have a team of strong people achieving a clear vision (Chapter 7).
- You encourage your team members to be all they can be for themselves, each other, and the organization (Chapter 8).

CHAPTER 1

LEADERS SURRENDER TO OTHERS' STRENGTHS

A horse will deliver the
strength you need when you believe
in the horse's strength.

A horse will deliver the strength you need when you believe in the horse's strength. Have you ever been surprised by someone exhibiting a strength or skill you never thought he or she had? Under what circumstances was the strength exhibited? Did you reinforce the strength to encourage its further development? We believe leadership is all about surrendering to others' strengths. When you give people time, space, belief (trust), and opportunity, you enable their strengths to surface.

Recall Tim's story of his trip up the mountain. Tim's horse had strengths Tim, as a young and inexperienced child, didn't understand. However, when Tim surrendered himself to his horse, it delivered all the strengths and resources Tim needed to get back to camp safely during the night.

In this book, we profess solution-focused leadership. We define solution-focused leadership this way: a solution-focused leader recognizes the strengths of those around him or her, encourages and affirms those strengths, harnesses them, and moves the team toward a mutual vision. In short, a solution-focused leader *surrenders to others' strengths*.

In the workplace, when we surrender to others' strengths, strengths we never knew about appear. Often, neither the leader nor the strengths' supplier would have said the supplier had those strengths. Therefore, one way for people to discover their own strengths and for a leader to recognize those strengths is for that leader to yield control, (sometimes) ask for help, and expect a required result to be achieved. Even without explicitly stating what the needed strengths are or how they must be applied, the leader allows people to reveal their strengths in meaningful ways. The person applying the strengths is encouraged to really take ownership of those strengths.

Many leaders believe leadership has a great deal to do with being in total control. They try to maintain complete control of situations, no matter what, by relying on only themselves to make all the important or significant decisions. A weak leader suppresses others' ability to have any control by making decisions for them, assuming, and many times demonstrating the belief that others' strengths are less important to the effort than the leader's strengths are. However, we have found a good leader maintains "control" in a wide variety of organizations and situations by allowing others, effectively, to control activities and decision making for which these others are responsible. When leaders allow others' decisions to affect a process, activity, or situation, others' strengths become evident. Thus, reassigning control often leads to revealing others' strengths. (See Chapter 4 for more insight into release and control.)

In our Solution-Focused Leadership program workshops, we've helped controlling leaders surrender to others' strengths during physical, mental, and emotional exercises. When such surrenders happen, those leaders feel great. They say things such as, "The surrendering was euphoric. That's the first time I let go of the burden of carrying everyone and everything on my shoulders." This feeling of euphoria helps leaders recognize, encourage, and affirm others' strengths.

As stated above, the Solution-Focused Leadership program focuses on two important ingredients: strengths and vision. Specifically, it encourages leaders to gather people's strengths and move those strengths collectively toward a mutual vision. In this chapter, we focus on strengths. In the next chapter, we focus on mutual vision.

When Tim and his horse were in the cold, dark mountains, their mutual vision was to reach the comfortable camp safely. Each wanted to reach the vision and supported the other party in doing so. Together, they could reach that vision – and did. This required reliance on the horse's strengths.

Understanding strengths is important because some people and organizations focus primarily on weaknesses without realizing it. Consider a training program in your organization or one you've encountered in your personal life. In and apart from these programs, do you plan and set up training that focuses on weaknesses or focuses on strengths? Remember, when you focus on weaknesses, you're doing damage control. When you focus on strengths, you're striving for excellence. You and your organization can contribute, succeed, and make a difference by delivering excellence through strengths. The more abundant an individual's or organization's strengths, the more plentiful the resulting excellence can be.

Sometimes, damage control is necessary. Indeed, in some circumstances, the existing or potential damage may be so great or so debilitating that focusing on weaknesses by reducing them is urgent and important. However, you will do better to control the damage as quickly, sufficiently, and efficiently as possible so you can turn your attention to developing strengths and achieving excellence.

What are your strengths? Answering this question is difficult for many people. Many of us don't think about our strengths. We just do what we do well and what works for us. Even so, do we know what our strengths are? Remember, as with Tim's horse, many times these strengths are hidden and must be revealed by circumstance or design. Do we know about strengths we have that other people don't know about? Are we so unaware of our strengths that they remain underutilized or unapplied to our everyday life? To prevent or change such a situation, try listing your strengths.

HORSE SENSE
If you have trouble recognizing your own strengths,
you'll have trouble recognizing others' strengths.

Remember, if you have trouble recognizing your own strengths, you'll have trouble recognizing others' strengths. Other people may be as reluctant or unable to advertise their strengths as you are. If you ask other people to list their strengths, they may have as much trouble making a list as you do. How do you get people to tell you their strengths when they don't know what those strengths are? Do you have to set up an extreme situation (such as being isolated on a mountaintop, in the cold darkness, far from home) for people to deliver strengths we may not normally think about? No. When you ask them about their exceptional moments, people will freely tell you their strengths (even strengths they couldn't list). In these inquiries, be specific: "Tell me about a time when you did [such and such] really well. How did you do that? What did you call upon inside yourself to help you be successful?" (For more information on exceptional moments, see Chapter 18.)

Solution-focused leaders are always looking for exceptional moments experienced by people around them. Over time, the leader realizes that each person can do something well – or at least better than usual – that can be applied to nearly any situation. By helping people identify and understand exceptional qualities in themselves in given situations, leaders ensure those people are better able to discover and define their strengths. The more someone recognizes he or she has exhibited personal strengths in the past, the more confidence that person will have in delivering those strengths in the future.

If we think about it, we realize horses have strengths we know we can depend on, such as having homing instincts. Horses also have strengths that cowboys know they can help develop. Jay Brewer, natural horse trainer of Wildcatter Ranch (just outside Graham, Texas), gives an example, citing the cowboy's ability to identify appropriate bloodlines of horses bred to work with cattle. A cowboy encourages the horse to do the work of a cattle horse, building on the animal's natural instinct, because he knows the horse has what it takes. The cowboy helps the horse develop "manners." For example, if the cowboy overfeeds the horse treats, he spoils the horse. The horse becomes "pushy and shovey" and does not respect the cowboy's space or authority.

In the workplace, leaders can develop overly familiar relationships with their direct reports (subordinates). As a result, a direct report who has become too familiar may also show "pushy and shovey" behavior, not respecting the leader's space or authority. As we'll discuss in the next chapter, leaders must distinguish between familiarity and intimacy in the workplace.

Jay Brewer offers another example of a cowboy helping a horse develop manners by addressing the horse's natural instinct, often considered a weakness, of eating whatever is available. If a cowboy gives a horse too much to eat, the horse will, like most animals, eat its food immediately and completely. We all know too much of anything can be dangerous and unhealthy. In creating a safe and healthy environment for his horse, the cowboy must guide it in proper manners and behavior, providing just the right amount of food required for strong, healthy horse development. As the cowboy develops a trusting relationship with his horse – by training, encouraging, and affirming the horse's efforts to develop its strengths – he remains aware of the horse's weaknesses, but doesn't dwell on them. Focusing on weakness is more likely to result in taking the heart out of the horse; it hinders the development of strengths. Acknowledging and accounting for weakness while providing for development and use of strengths is much more likely to result in growing the horse's heart (desire and caring and wanting to contribute). (See Chapter 7 for further discussion of the importance of what you focus on.)

So, in your workplace, how are you developing relationships with your direct reports? What are you doing to focus on people's strengths?

CHAPTER 2

PEOPLE NATURALLY SEEK LEADERSHIP

Horses naturally seek leadership.

Horses naturally seek leadership. We believe people do too. People look for and are drawn to individuals who emit qualities of leadership. However, we also believe that while true leaders may seem natural, very few individuals are born leaders. Leaders must work continuously at leadership to improve.

We define leadership as the ability to recognize, encourage, affirm, and gather others' strengths so a group can move toward a shared vision. This definition, which aligns with solution-focused leadership, is centered on strengths, encouragement, and vision. Most importantly, this definition is other-centered, not self-centered. In previous years, people saw leadership as being about the leader: the leader's competence, charisma, and passion. Leaders still need to be technically and socially competent, have character and integrity, and be passionate about vision and success. However, true leadership today also must include intimacy. Leaders must have profound and intimate knowledge of their people, and of the organization's work, vision, and clients.

Being other-centered doesn't come naturally. People are born selfish and very few totally mature out of self-centeredness. True leadership requires us to put aside our personal needs and desires, and to focus on others. In this way, leaders can help others bring their strengths, thoughts, and feelings to the surface, thus developing their readiness, willingness, and ability to interact with their leaders in order to achieve a shared vision.

When Tim's grandpa released control to the horses so they could carry his grandsons and him home, he was other-focused in two ways. First, he knew the horses had a homing strength. Second, he remained aware of a shared vision: getting home safely. In his moment of need, Tim's grandpa didn't have to explain his vision, because he had developed trusting relationships with the horses and with his grandsons.

As Jay Brewer says, "A *good* horse trainer can *make* a horse do what you *want*. A great horse trainer can get a horse to want to do what you want." That kind of skill is not just natural training or natural horsemanship. It's true leadership. As Ray Hunt writes in *Cowboy Logic*, "Let your idea become the horse's idea." Horses and people prefer and work harder to develop ideas they own. A leader's job is to help horses, or people, own the ideas and behaviors that ultimately contribute to their shared vision. The most effective way for horses and people to own ideas and behavior is for them to understand they have strengths they can contribute to the ideas and behaviors that will bring the vision to success.

Take another look at the illustration that accompanies this chapter. In this image, the cowboy knows what he wants. His job is to translate his vision of what he wants into the horse's actions. To do so, the cowboy needs to know clearly and specifically what he wants. At that point he'll be prepared to undertake the necessary step of communicating his vision to the horse.

In the business world, what's needed to accomplish the same goal (communicating a vision to the people who will help you achieve it)? First, leaders gain attention through having a clear vision. Second, they give meaning by communicating the vision. Third, they build trust by positioning themselves to accomplish the vision. Finally, and fourth, they build confidence through having a healthy understanding of success and failure.

In this chapter's illustration, the cowboy already has a vision. Because he's getting the horse to behave in the manner needed to accomplish the vision, we can assume he must have communicated that vision to the horse. The cowboy has also positioned both the horse and himself to accomplish the vision. He communicates assurance and direction to the horse through his grip on the reins and his seat in the saddle. In turn, the horse feels the cowboy's confidence in heading in the right direction.

HORSE SENSE

The cowboy communicates assurance and direction
to the horse through his grip on the reins and his seat in the saddle.
In turn, the horse feels the cowboy's confidence
in heading in the right direction.

When natural-horse-trainer cowboys work with a horse, their thinking is totally outside themselves; instead, they focus on the horse. They mentally and emotionally go to wherever the horse is and relate that place to their vision. Similarly, in the workplace, by developing a vision and encouraging all our people to contribute to that vision, we lead effectively.

We strongly encourage anyone who wants to be a true leader to read Buck Brannaman's book *The Faraway Horses*. The book is about Buck's life, which is interesting in and of itself. Yet reading this book helps people understand what *other-focused* really means. Being other-focused is more subtle and profound than it seems initially. Buck shows his other-focus in three ways: first, and mostly, through his relationships with his horses; second, through his relationships with the horse owners; and third, through guiding the relationships of horse owners with their horses.

Given these credentials, it's no wonder Buck inspired Nicholas Evans's book, *The Horse Whisperer*, which led to the movie of the same title. In *The Faraway Horses*, Buck writes:

> The term *horse whisperer* was first used in ancient
> Scotland, but since the novel and the movie, the phrase has

been used to describe trainers who have developed methods of working respectfully and gently with horses. It defines what I do for a living. It's not a bad definition, but it's incomplete and somewhat misleading.

I observe the horse, learn from him, and remember the experience. Then I try to find a way to use what I've learned to fit in with what I'd like the horse to do. These are the techniques that I learned from men like Tom Dorrance, Ray Hunt, and others who were using them long before I ever did.

My own story is about horses, and I guess it's a love story too. I do the things I do when I work with horses because I just plain love them.

Buck succeeds in his work with horses because he "love[s] them." Similarly, true leadership requires more than what you'd give to a role, a responsibility, or a job. True leadership is a calling. In fact, we believe to lead well, you must love – that is, you must be able to accurately assess another person's needs. (We also address leadership and love in Chapter 17.)

Leadership also requires learning with curiosity. Through a passion for loving and learning with curiosity, we can become other-focused leaders. We can learn about and reinforce others' strengths.

A true leader takes success and failure in stride. Leaders do their very best in the moment and continually strive to improve, all while influencing those around them to do the same. In guiding a team or horse toward the shared vision, leaders recognize and reward small successes. Failures are accepted, as both the cowboy and the horse or the supervisor and workers learn lessons.

Yet, while incorporating other-focus, true leadership begins with introspection. First, leaders have to observe, assess, and supervise themselves as they make decisions. To evaluate themselves, they should find the answers to questions such as the following:

- Who am I?
- Where am I?
- What means most to me?
- What are my strengths and where did they come from?
- What do I need to improve?
- What defines my character?

Your character is the kind of person you are when nobody's looking. A successful leader looks deeply inward to discover how he or she influences others. In today's world, we can seldom *make* a person do something, but we can *influence* the person to believe in and do that thing.

True leadership also requires personal mastery. Leadership requires leaders to know themselves very well, including their strengths and weaknesses. When leaders understand themselves intimately, they're better able to develop and grow in ways that support those who work with them. Such personal mastery takes huge effort. Yet, as a leader, the organization for which you work and your people's well-being both depend on your personal mastery.

While a true leader is competent enough to complete the work at hand and to make good decisions, he or she also has passion and is comfortable with intimacy. A true leader has integrity, courage, and exemplary character. In other words, he or she has the highest-level values.

Louis Wood, natural horse trainer of Mountainview Ranch just outside Waynesboro, Virginia, suggests an additional important effect of good leadership as it relates to horse training: "When the horse realizes you're offering leadership, it will relax." Similarly, in the workplace, people will contribute their best when they feel less stressed and are more relaxed. Being relaxed doesn't mean being asleep or unmotivated; instead, it indicates feeling comfortable in the situation and confident about oneself. People perform more thoughtfully when they're calm. A horse may not think the way people do, but it will respond to a leader with helpful, instinctive actions more effectively when it's relaxed – and people will too.

Shared vision, personal mastery, and focusing on others support cowboys and horses in building effective and lasting relationships that foster trust and result in success. Trusting, lasting, and successful workplace relationships will also result in greater organizational performance when leaders are able to apply these principles to their daily interactions and decision making.

CHAPTER 3

START THE RELATIONSHIP BY SPENDING TIME LISTENING

Upon first meeting a horse, a cowboy
spends time listening.

U pon first meeting a horse, a cowboy spends time listening. Listening accomplishes many things. It:

- creates connections;
- promotes learning;
- honors and lifts up others;
- ensures effective information transfers; and
- demonstrates respect for others.

Connecting to, acknowledging, and learning about a person (or a horse) all help build new and better relationships in which strengths come to the surface. We abide by the following principle: whenever you start a relationship, you should spend time listening. We interpret this principle to mean that the periods when a relationship begins and when individuals make a change in an existing relationship are the two most critical times in working or living together. At all times, but especially during these periods, how well you listen is a good indication of the relationship's ultimate value. In fact, listening effectively may be the most important skill you'll ever learn for your life and work.

Oral communication has two parts: speaking or sending, and listening or receiving. Remember, communication is transferring information; good information is required for good decision making, and good decision making equals good management. Good management leads to good supervision, good leadership, and good facilitation. It also gives us leaders the opportunity to be good in other roles we play in the workplace. Whenever we send an oral message, we indicate our meaning through a number of signs: the content (the words), tone of voice, facial expression, and body language. Facial expressions and body language are relatively important whenever people send messages. Because of this, when we receive messages, we may listen more with our eyes than with our ears.

In other words, we can listen to a horse that doesn't speak; we also need to listen attentively to a person who does speak. Consider speaking and listening. Listening is the power position. This may seem counterintuitive, but it's also true. If you are listening effectively, you can lead the other person (or horse) to wherever he or she needs to go. Often this destination can be different from where you expected to go. The idea of listening effectively is especially important in dealing with internal or external clients, because in those cases, wherever the other person needs or wants to go is typically more important than where you'd like the other person to go.

Jay Brewer, of Wildcatter Ranch just outside Graham, Texas, says we need to listen to a horse with our eyes. We need to read the horse's body language. For example, when a horse is colicky, the horse tips his nose to his stomach or lies down. This is an instinctive reaction on the horse's part. The horse trainer or the cowboy has to learn to read the horse – determining whether the horse is demonstrating signs of ill health, for example – if the situation is to be improved.

The key to listening is in focusing on the other person. When listening, we need to shut off our inner voices and encourage other people to speak. We want to receive their messages and we send signals to them demonstrating their importance to us. We reflect the importance of what is being said; we make a place where the other people in our conversation feel empowered. Ultimately, listening is the leadership position because *listening facilitates empowerment*. We lead by encouraging other people to contribute at their best, and this encouragement is facilitated through attentive listening.

HORSE SENSE

The key to listening is in focusing on the other person.

A SUNNY SOLUTION

We can use the acronym SOLAR as a memory device for attentive listening practices.

S is for *square*. Squarely face the other person. Be attentive, tune in, and face the person to whom you're listening.

O is for *open*. Use open body language and have an open mind. An open mind means silencing your own inner voice so you can hear the other person's voice.

L is for *lean forward*. By leaning forward, you engage the other person and signal your interest in connecting for communication.

A is for *appropriate eye contact*. In American culture, this means making eye contact about 80 percent of the time.

R is for *reflection*. Don't let information go in one ear and out the other. In other words, *R* can also stand for *receptive*, which is what you should be when given the chance to share ideas. And there's one other *R*: relaxed. Take it easy when you're talking with somebody. Make it a pleasant experience, not a small drama. It's hard to communicate when you're uptight. To truly reflect on what you are hearing, you need to be energized but comfortable.

Consider the concept of reflection, as in the literal idea of using a mirror.

While there are a great variety of listening skills, the most powerful one is reflection. Reflection means thinking about what you hear, demonstrating attentiveness, and engaging and encouraging thoughtfully. These are the tools you need to use to elicit the best in another and to harvest the wisdom and usefulness of what is being given to you.

The reflection process is also how people silence their inner voices. In conversation, focus on absorbing the total message the other person is sending through his or her words, tone of voice, body language, and facial expression. Maintain a 45 percent aural focus and a 55 percent visual focus. Concentrating on someone else's total message means the listener's inner voice tends to take second place. During the conversation, try to capture the speaker's emotions. Reflect by saying something such as, "It sounds as if you're [excited, sad, disappointed] because [of what you're saying]."

Remember the following key points about reflection:
- Reflection honors the other participants in the conversation.
- Reflection helps them clarify their thoughts and feelings.
- Reflection creates a safe place where the other participants in the conversation may be willing to go more deeply into the real issues, as opposed to sharing the superficial statements people typically use to open conversations. (For example, an angry outburst is usually superficial in that the anger is covering up a real issue and emotion, such as disappointment, hurt, or sadness.)

- Reflection helps reduce communication redundancy, which means speakers talk on and on because they don't believe those listening really understand the message. So they deliver the message over and over. This redundancy is eliminated through reflection because the listener captures the message the first time through.

When you're starting to build a relationship with another person, reflection is probably the most helpful of all skills you can use. Reflection is useful for validating both your thinking and your understanding of the message you're receiving from the other person.

Monty Roberts, author of *Horse Sense for People*, writes, "A good trainer can hear a horse talk to him. A great trainer can hear a horse whisper to him." Isn't that curious? Obviously, the horse doesn't talk. Even so, a great trainer and perhaps even a good trainer can receive the horse's message. The implication here is powerful. Words may be the least useful part of the message being communicated. If the listener is being other-focused (for the cowboy, horse-focused), words aren't necessary to understand three things: first, how ready and willing the other individual is to act; second, what the action will be; and third, what the intended result is. In the workplace, when you're tuned in to other people, they will be able to recognize if you're reflecting by how you respond emotionally. Reflection helps people feel encouraged and empowered. Therefore, start each relationship with an other-focused frame of mind. Otherwise, you'll exert a great deal of effort trying to recover from potentially untrue behaviors, statements, or decisions that suggest the other person doesn't matter to you.

There's even more to applying the principle of listening to relationships. Spend some time beginning, changing, and improving your relationships, all while listening actively. Remember, a relationship doesn't remain constant. Once a relationship has been initiated, changes are always happening, whether you feel good, bad, or indifferent about those changes. If you want to improve your relationships, *listen more*. Although you can't force your listening on someone, we've found you don't have to do much to get someone to talk. Listening involves having a responsive attitude. You can only respond by listening when someone else speaks. As you learn how to listen better, you naturally encourage others to speak.

HORSE SENSE
As you learn how to listen better, you naturally
encourage others to speak.

Now, let's consider the speaking position in communication. How does a cowboy speak to his horse? In the United States, the horse doesn't understand English, but responds to English words; yet in France, the horse responds to French words. Horses do not understand language, of course; instead, they understand the connection between a sound, a movement, or a look, and what they have been trained to do (or would instinctively do) when that sound, movement, or look occurs.

In *Cowboy Logic*, Ray Hunt writes, "The horse will teach you if you'll *Listen*." Ray capitalizes the word Listen because the person doing the listening is in the leadership role. In Tim's story about coming down from the mountaintop, the group survived because Tim's grandpa "Listened" to the horses. Grandpa had developed a relationship of trust. Because he was able to become other-focused, he was able to recognize the strengths needed to get them home. Without much "asking," Tim's grandpa enabled the horses to carry out their part in achieving the shared vision.

When leading people, you may take on a directing role, or a *judging role*, when you ask closed questions. (Closed questions take either a yes or no response, or begin with the word *why*.) Using a directing role can lead you to judge (and misjudge) others. At times, directing is appropriate and necessary: for example, Grandpa told Tim and Tracey what to do to get off the mountain. At that moment, Grandpa was *directing*, not leading. His action wasn't about others' strengths; the action was about Grandpa's strengths (which, in turn, included recognizing the horses' strengths).

In order to direct and judge less, adopt a learning posture. You take on a learning role or posture when you ask open questions (questions beginning with the words *what* or *how*). The people you lead will appreciate your desire to learn. Because of that appreciation, strengths will emerge frequently, seemingly out of nowhere. Listening helps a leader understand, and understanding is power.

CHAPTER 4
UNDERSTANDING COMES
BEFORE CONTROL

Don't fight with the horse; instead, help
the horse understand what you want.

Don't fight with the horse; instead, help the horse understand what you want. At their core, horses and people want to do the right thing (recall the discussions about natural horsemanship or the Theory Y approach to supervision); they don't want to balk or fight. At the same time, each player in a situation wants to be in control of him- or herself. Fighting, with either a horse or a person, is about control, force, and submission. Fighting with a horse can be a losing proposition. Imagine a person sitting on an almost-one-ton horse fighting to get that horse to do what the person wants. At times, you may have felt as if you were fighting with some of your people in your workplace. You knew what was needed, the proper steps, and the constraints. If people had done what you wanted based on what you knew, you could have efficiently and effectively gotten to where you needed to be. To diffuse a situation and rebalance the scene so each player can regain proper footing and focus on the mutual vision, a cowboy needs to ensure his horse understands what he wants and that this want is aligned with their shared vision. The same goes for leaders and their supervisees in the workplace.

After a cowboy gets into a push-and-shove interaction with his horse, there are certainly times he feels like the man in this chapter's illustration. Similarly, after push-and-shove interactions, those of us who supervise others sometimes feel as beaten up as we would have had we been in a physical fight, even though those we supervise may not be physically larger or stronger than we are. However, the individuals we supervise may well have advantages in a rough-and-tumble interaction. They typically know the work process more intimately than their leaders do. Sometimes they also know the client and their coworkers better. The advantages they have over their leaders may also be strengths those leaders need to recognize, understand, and access. Remember, the wise leader looks for strengths in his or her team. In Tim's story, the horses' strengths – their ability to see at night and their homing instinct – emerged because the horses were closer to the process, or vision, of returning to camp. Grandpa's wisdom came from being other-focused and thus knowing the others' strengths.

We all want to control our destiny and our performance. However, when destiny and performance depend on others, our desire to control the situation can get in our way. As we discussed in Chapter 1, Solution-focused leadership is based on the premise that a leader surrenders to others' strengths. Surrendering to others requires leaders to put aside their desire for personal control.

You can't control a horse unless it allows you to do so. The horse is too big and too strong. Some cowboys get horses to allow control by using punishment and fear. Some supervisors also gain control over subordinates by using fear. Fear as a control tactic works to a certain level in certain circumstances with certain people. In fact, it works well enough to encourage some people to continue to use the tactic. However, as a leader, you will achieve more productivity through using trust and mutual respect than you will from using fear. Encouragement is a far more powerful tool than fear. That's because favorable attitudes breed more favorable results. Fear breeds more fear, hurt, anger, and dissatisfaction. Plus, the workday is more pleasant and the partnership is more cordial when leaders give encouragement. (We'll discuss the importance of encouragement in Chapter 8.)

HORSE SENSE
You can't control a horse unless it allows you to do so.

Traditional horse trainers use Theory X and bank on fear to subdue a horse. Natural horse trainers embrace Theory Y and are aware of a horse's tendencies toward fear. Instead, they strive to make the horse feel safe, thereby building a relationship based on trust. In *The Man Who Listens to Horses*, Monty Roberts describes the difference in approaches to horse training, contrasting his father's practice of the traditional, violent method, with his own, new method:

> "Horses understand one thing only," my father barked, "and that is fear. If you do not hurt them first, they will hurt you."
>
> I had come to think of my process as entirely different from that of "breaking" horses. That word has connotations of violence and domination ... I changed the nomenclature. From that day on, I called my method "starting" horses. If traditional breaking was designed to generate fear in the horse, I wanted to create trust ... In short, instead of telling young horses "You must," I wanted to ask them, "Will you?"

Most people react to (or act upon) only what they understand a situation to be or involve. Their perception of reality versus the leader's actual reality is irrelevant to their actions, since they don't necessarily understand other people's realities. People effectively act on what they understand. They want and need to understand what's expected of them. Moreover, they want to understand where they're headed and what the necessary steps to get there are. If leaders want people to respond to them, they must work at getting those people to understand not only their realities (giving people pertinent information at the right time), but also what the leaders expect their subordinates to do.

Given our observations of natural horse trainers, we believe understanding on the part of the horse includes a buy-in by that horse. In the workplace, when a person buys into where you're going and how to get there, the person gains understanding of the situation. When the person has understanding, the situation is under control. In this discussion, *control* means to hold the situation steady and keep it stable. Many people can contribute to a situation being under control, which invites plenty of buying-in. This method of control leads to comfort and motivation, not demand and domination.

As Ray Hunt writes in *Cowboy Logic*, "The slower you go, the faster you'll learn." Attitude, pace, and starting point are elemental in placing understanding before control. Sometimes cowboys and leaders have to slow down to the horses' or workers' pace. Doing so ensures the cowboys and leaders know what the horses or workers understand and carefully consider where the horses or workers are in terms of understanding what's expected, how to do what's expected, and who should do what.

Consider the following principle from natural horse trainer Louis Wood, which highlights the ideas of placing and pacing to achieve a vision: "You must work at the horse's pace ... work your horse where it is, not where you'd like for it to be." Examine your own place and pace. First, at what *place* do you work? Where are you and where are the other people (physically and figuratively)? Those other people might be subordinates, colleagues, or clients, but if their understanding and ability aren't at a place where they can respond to your expectations, you must start where those people are and build the understanding and ability they need from there. Expecting other people to be at different places from where they *actually* are gets you nowhere.

Second, at what *pace* do you work? If you outstrip the people you need alongside you, you'll be dealing with a gap between you, not with being productive. The objective is not for any party to feel superior; rather, all parties should feel compatible. To know the place and pace to establish when meeting the people you're expecting to work with you, it's necessary to listen with both your eyes and ears.

Natural horse trainers believe trainers should not use pain through a bit to control horses, nor should they fight with the horses. In a fight with a horse or person, the leader is trying to exert power to gain an advantage over the situation, to control the situation, and to influence its outcome. The key to success is shared power, especially when working with a horse much bigger and stronger than a cowboy. In such scenarios, the cowboy learns to use his powers of understanding, experience, and imagination to guide the horse's powers of instinct and physical strength.

So, what can you take away from this?

- You must align your expectations with reality.
- You must communicate expectations, but can't expect people to be places they aren't.
- You have to focus on those you work with, so you know who and where they are.

When these three points have been achieved, you can encourage others to join you in a spirit of collaboration, contribution, and productivity.

Being a true leader involves being other-focused. In Tim's story, Grandpa had to focus on the horses and on his grandsons. In the workplace, a leader has to focus on the client. At the same time, the leader also has to focus on the boss and the owners, his or her peers, and those he or she is responsible for. Leaders must focus on those they intend to lead, since by being other-focused leaders can understand where and who their people are. Only then will they be more apt to be successful and cultivate productive and enduring relationships with their leaders. Though leaders can get some productivity through threat, fear, pain, and control, they can achieve even more productivity and excellence through caring, trust, comfort, and shared power.

A trainer friend of Tim's once said it's important to value the long-term over the short-term. If you approach a horse with the attitude of making him do what you want, or showing him you're the boss, he may behave – at first. However, over time, his mind won't lean toward partnership ideas. In fact, you should expect the opposite. The horse will be thinking, "As soon as I can, I'll show you!" He'll look to separate himself from you and from the job as soon as possible.

In sum, value understanding before and over control. You need to understand your people. You also need to communicate your vision and expectations clearly, so your people understand what's needed. If you do that, we hope ending up like the cowboy in this chapter's illustration will be a thing of the past for you.

CHAPTER 5
PEOPLE'S STRENGTHS DIRECTLY REFLECT THEIR UNIQUENESS

No two horses are exactly alike.

N o two horses are exactly alike. That's true for people too. We shouldn't expect any person to be a certain way. We might expect people to be what we want them to be or to be just like us, to think as we do, and behave the way we'd like. Yet all people are wonderfully different. These differences give leaders the opportunity to assemble and develop work teams more powerful than the sum of their individuals. In such cases, how do leaders get the most and the best out of their people?

The problem (or, perhaps, the opportunity or challenge) is simple: what makes sense to some people doesn't necessarily make sense to everyone else. Leaders often wish they could "fix" people so everything makes sense to everyone. However, in fixing another person, it's debatable whether a leader is trying to fix the situation, his or her relationship with the person, or the other person's attitude, desire, and commitment. Well, you can't fix any of these things, because you can't change another person. Other people have to want to change themselves. So, how do you get to a place where other people want to change and will work toward doing so in order to benefit themselves and the situation? First, you need to consider whether or not those others are in the best place for change, based on their own unique strengths and experience.

However, before we go further, there's one very important thing to remember: in most cases, you shouldn't need to change a person. Instead, you should try to discover that person's special uniqueness and use it. By searching for, encouraging, and affirming a person's hidden strengths – their traits, talents, experience, or knowledge – you might discover in that person someone different from the individual you thought you knew. In your eyes that person has changed. However, you were not the cause of that change. Rather, you changed *yourself* by changing your perception of that other person. In doing so, you changed your reality and increased your understanding – and understanding is power. According to bestselling author and leadership expert Stephen Covey, when you change your perception of someone, you can influence that person to change and be more in line with your viewpoint. (Part of supervision is working with change, and we discuss change in Chapter 13.)

In the illustration that accompanies this chapter, a cowboy moves a bushel basket and finds, underneath it, that his horse has hidden strengths. The cowboy has to remove an obstacle, which changes his perception about the horse. This idea transfers easily to the workplace. People don't always realize they have strengths, let alone know what those strengths are. Indeed, while all of us have strengths, we don't always acknowledge their presence or recognize them for what they are. To overcome this mindset, try listing all your strengths. Next, underline those strengths, identifying them as either helpful in your current workplace or as transferrable to many settings (for example, your home, community, or many other types of work). Defining and categorizing your strengths may be difficult at first, but it is a very useful exercise over time.

While we suggested the exercise of listing your strengths and the importance of recognizing the strengths of those around us in Chapter 1, we believe these ideas are important enough to reaffirm, and we believe a leader will help people bring hidden strengths to the surface, as illustrated in this chapter. Indeed, a leader's job is to help his or her people recognize their strengths, be proud of them, and effectively use them when needed. If leaders help people discover, develop, and display hidden strengths, they are leaders who help people reach their full potential. As in this chapter's illustration, in many cases people keep their strengths hidden (under a figurative bushel basket). In effect, a good leader searches for and lifts the bushel baskets, thus revealing people's strengths. The effort of helping people bring strengths to the surface – especially strengths they may not realize they possess – is one of the greatest contributions to the workplace a leader can make.

Let's return to the story that begins Part I of this book. When they were isolated up on the mountain that night, Tim's grandpa knew the party's horses had strengths he and his grandsons needed to use. The horses couldn't explain their strengths to Tim and Tracey. Yet, by allowing the horses to carry them back to camp, the boys helped the horses show their strengths and resources clearly. In addition, the strengths and resources within the horses were acknowledged, and the boys learned from and about the horses.

A leader helps each team member understand, appreciate, respect, and relate to the strengths of the others, thereby demonstrating the team's collective strengths. You might wonder how you can support people in finding their own strengths and resources, which will enable them to move the group or endeavor closer to the vision. Focus, for a moment, on that vision. A good vision combines a dream with action, and a clear, challenging, and desirable vision helps a leader's people feel self-assured about the future. To bring your vision into focus, you can consider writing a vision statement. By writing a vision statement, you clarify your vision (the vision in your mind) and you have a tangible reference point to aid your focus. (You can find an exercise for crafting your personal vision on the following website: www.newportgroupllc.com.)

In *Cowboy Logic*, Ray Hunt writes, "You need to have a picture in your mind of what you want your horse to do." Think back to the illustration in Chapter 2, in which the cowboy does exactly what Hunt states. Like this cowboy, the picture in your mind *is* your vision. Having your vision clearly in mind is the starting point. You must figure out how to communicate that vision so clearly and precisely the person (or horse) you're working with will have the same picture in his or her mind.

While that's the foundation, building that foundation isn't easy. Leaders need to understand how they can combine team members' collective strengths as they work together to achieve the vision without losing each individual's uniqueness. First, leaders have to know where they're going themselves as managers, supervisors, and, especially, leaders, in terms of the vision. They must fully understand the vision in relation to their own work. Then, they have to focus on their team.

Often, people in work units will challenge the team vision, basing that challenge either on their individual fears and insecurities or on confidence in their own strengths. If leaders listen carefully to each challenge, they'll understand more about each person's needs and how they can support their people both individually and collectively. Also, if leaders believe (as we, the authors, do) that each person is uniquely creative, within their team they will undoubtedly find nuggets of wisdom for refining their vision or, at least, refining their strategy for achieving the vision.

In the end, good leaders will identify what their people need from them. Some team members will need encouragement, praise, detailed instructions, or freedom to explore. Others will want to understand the vision and then be left alone to apply their strengths and resources, according to their own way of doing things, to achieving the vision. For leaders, matching responses to each person's needs will take time but, ultimately, will result in success. Good supervisors and leaders will prioritize identifying and matching resources to required tasks under their purview.

To succeed in leadership, recognize your team members' different strengths, resources, and personalities (including their ways of perceiving the world, and processing and acting on those perceptions). We all know people are quite different from one another. Don't decide who a person is based on who you want the person to be. Don't decide what a person needs in terms of who he or she actually is. You can't make a trotter out of a Clydesdale. Allow people to be who they are; understand, accept, and even celebrate their different personalities.

Unfortunately, occasionally one or two of your people won't be able to move forward, which will cause friction and difficulty among the work team. The people in question may not want to move forward, or they may not be equipped or capable to do so. After a good effort on your part to alleviate their fears and insecurities, you may need to move those people to other assignments more in line with their strengths. Otherwise, these people may wear down the other team members and reduce group productivity. As a leader, the kind – and fair – thing to do is help any and all of your people find the best match for their strengths, desires, and their job responsibilities, even if that means leaving your workplace for a different setting more in line with their strengths and interests.

Both supervisors and cowboys can work with their team's inherent strengths to achieve success. In *True Horsemanship through Feel*, Bill Dorrance discusses the need for a trainer to capitalize on a horse's basic nature and sensitivity. He states:

> To help the horse learn to understand what you want, you can make use of his nature. He is naturally curious and is apt to investigate things he hasn't seen or been around before. He is also liable to run away from those same things. There's a spot somewhere in between [those tendencies] where an observing person can develop some skill at blending in [his/her] plan for how he/she wants the horse to maneuver with the horse's willingness to do these things for a person. We can work with a horse this way because it's part of the horse's basic nature to want to get along.

Most people are the same: they want to get along. So, as a supervisor, try to find the "spot somewhere in between;" that way, you too can move your people along toward reaching shared goals. At the same time, you'll be able to encourage your team members' individual growth and help them develop unique natural gifts, talents, and learned skill sets.

Many years ago, Harold's wife told their family physician about how Harold's coworkers were constantly anticipating his heart attack. They imagined Harold would have a heart attack if he continued his hard-driving attitude and behavior. In reply, the physician reminded Harold's wife of the differentiation between racehorses and workhorses. "Racehorses are different from workhorses," he said. "You don't want to race a workhorse or work a racehorse. Harold's a racehorse. He'll be fine racing. He shouldn't try to be something he isn't." Clearly, Harold shouldn't change who he is and nor should anyone else. Instead, others should acknowledge and celebrate people's unique attitudes and strengths.

There are many different types of horses – and different types of people – we get to work with. Perhaps it's easier to categorize horses. Racehorses are used primarily for sport. Workhorses, in the cowboy's context, are used for working cattle and performing other tasks around a ranch. Other types of horses include draft horses, which are bred for hard, heavy tasks such as plowing and farm labor.

Because no two people have the same experiences in life or the same inclinations at birth, each person's mental models (a mental model is something through which a person filters all incoming sensory data to produce thoughts and feelings) are unique. As a result, each person has a unique understanding of any event or situation, and each person has different motivations. Some seek tangible rewards and others seek self-satisfaction. Leaders need to know the differences among their people in order to determine how to treat individuals fairly while acknowledging their differences.

Determining the best ways to motivate people may be more difficult than determining motivations for horses. Jay Brewer explains, "I don't think horses think in terms of rewards." Perhaps horses don't think in terms of cause and effect, or in terms of rewards being a consequence of good behavior. However, some cowboys use the carrot-and-stick approach (literally) when dealing with horses. The carrot-and-stick approach is called "extrinsic motivation." Total-quality-management guru W. Edwards Deming states that when dealing with people, leaders need to work exclusively with intrinsic motivation; significantly, *extrinsic* motivation drives out intrinsic motivation.

Often, leaders consider the work and accomplishments of those they're responsible for to be part of the workers' regular duties. Therefore, a leader may not feel compelled to reward team members for what they should be doing as part of their job descriptions. Also, when a team member tries something for the first time with dubious results, the leader may not feel compelled to reward the person. Instead, a strong leader learns people need to be encouraged, affirmed, and appreciated, even for actions that seem obvious or are good efforts toward a less-than-successful result.

HORSE SENSE

A strong leader knows people need to be encouraged, affirmed, and appreciated, even for actions that seem obvious or are good efforts toward a less-than-successful result.

The idea of a reward for a person isn't necessarily as obvious as a carrot for a horse. Instead, consider the idea of a reward as approval, affirmation, appreciation, or acknowledgment. Sometimes, we call this type of affirmation a workplace "attaboy." Big, tangible rewards (such as bonuses) can be a mixed blessing. A person receiving a tangible reward may feel encouraged by it, but he or she may also feel guilty, or believe he or she doesn't deserve the reward more than others do. Another person who sees and does not receive the reward may become unmotivated, especially if he or she believes the reward should have gone to him or her. However, small, less-tangible rewards can be distributed freely. For example, genuine, small affirmations and encouragements can lead to more helpful results when bestowed upon all members of the work team.

In dealing with work team (or even family) situations, our advice is to reward even modest efforts in the direction you want. If a team or family member happens to do something expected of him or her but seldom achieved, reward the slightest attempt. You may think the expected effort doesn't deserve reward; after all, it's expected. You might respond, "It's about time you did [the thing you should have done long ago]." Instead, try saying, "Thanks for doing what you did; your effort really helps me." This affirmation, given even for the slightest attempt, encourages the person to perform the same, expected effort again. Affirmation feels good and people want to do what leads to feeling good. Feeling good builds confidence. Over time, if you continue with affirmation, that person's expected effort may become a habit, and you'll get the regular and frequent effort you wanted all along.

CHAPTER 6
A LEADER HARNESSES OTHERS' STRENGTHS

A draft horse considers a harness helpful when getting ready to work.

A draft horse considers a harness helpful when getting ready to work. A harness provides the horse with support, guidance, and direction. Think about your organization. What materials, systems, and procedures are in place to support your people's work? Which do you think might restrain them? How do you know the difference?

Consider the importance of the harness to a draft horse. While we can learn lessons from different types of horses, in this chapter we focus on draft horses. Typically, draft horses are worked "in harness." A *harness*, to a draft horse, is a wonderful thing. More broadly, the meaning of harness includes the concepts of both restraint and support. Generally, *support* has a favorable connotation. *Restraint* is more complex, since it is only considered favorable in certain situations.

In *Taking the Reins*, when we consider recognizing, encouraging, and affirming strengths as critical ingredients of solution-focused leadership, we want leaders to "harness" the strengths and voluntary energies of their organizations' team members. First, a good leader relies on building the right kinds of relationships with those being led, since a good relationship is the foundation from which favorable outcomes emerge. (We discuss what we call enduring relationships in the "Final Thoughts" chapter.)

It's fitting to use the word *harness* to describe gathering others' strengths to help achieve a purpose. While *harness* may refer to directing disparate strengths to work in harmony, the word also conjures up the image of a draft horse wearing its leather straps, buckles, gear, or tackle, all of which enables the large animal to pull a wagon or an old-time farm implement. The process of harnessing, which is used to access the draft horse's pulling power, seems pretty straightforward, doesn't it? Even so, this image fails to educate us about what's going on beneath the surface of the harnessing concept. Whether you lead people or horses, those being led must voluntarily give some strengths, attitudes, and behaviors. Of course, what a leader desires from those he or she leads is not just their time; a leader also desires team members' hearts and minds, intelligence and creativity, and drive and resourcefulness. Optimizing these strengths only happens when those strengths are volunteered.

The horses bringing Tim, Tracey, and their grandpa safely home in the dark weren't draft horses and didn't have harnesses. However, the horses did have supports they relied upon and that showed them how to succeed. For example, when Tim got on his horse, his grandpa instructed him to use the reins: "Just tie the reins together, so they don't fall; then, we'll lie down in the saddles, put our arms around the horses' necks, and let them go." These actions supported the horses, which then got the family home safely. Remember, the horses and the humans had a shared vision of getting home (that is, to the campsite). The horses' visions were connected to the vision of the family, because Grandpa and the horses were thinking alike: we need to get home safely. When they felt the storm coming, the horses didn't run away or buck. They remained calm and used the support of loose reins and their homing strength to get back to safety.

Not surprisingly, when asked about what makes them effective with horses, good horsemen don't start with the techniques or the skills the job requires. Instead, they talk first about the more abstract relationships they have with the animals. You might be thinking, "What? Don't they simply make the horse do what they want the horse to do? Aren't they the bosses? Heck, they're the humans, right?"

There's a little truth in some of those questions. However, unless the cowboy starts by building a relationship of trust and a partner-ship with the horse, the final outcome will be less than satisfying, at best; at worst, the relationship could end in disaster. The cowboy wants the horse's heart, as well as its body, to be committed to the tasks he asks of it.

The same distinction applies in the workplace. When consider-ing the goal or objective as a supervisor assigns a task, W. Edwards

Deming, the total-quality-management guru, asks, "By what method?" His point is profound. Having a goal or objective only works when the leader or supervisor supplies team members with the means that make their success possible. It's essential to have a method that will produce the results called for by the goal or objective.

HORSE SENSE

Having a goal or objective only works when the leader supplies team members with the means that make their success possible.

Think again about the questions posed in the beginning of this chapter. Now, add to them. How might you begin to gain your people's hearts? How might you go about learning which materials and processes are supporting work and which are restraining?

In ages past, when manual labor constituted much of the work to be accomplished, leaders were interested in securing people's hands (or perhaps their backs) to build a Great Wall or Pyramid. As time went on, leaders found they wanted both their team members' hands and heads. Leaders needed the team members' thinking strengths to guide those hands. Today, to stay competitive in the global, 24/7/365 marketplace, we need more than people's hands and heads. We need their hearts: their commitment, dedication, energy, and spirit. People work best and most productively when their hearts are in the work.

So, what motivates people to give leaders their hearts? Well, good leaders provide people with support while building relationships based on trust and genuine caring. Just as a draft horse recognizes a harness as support – not as a restraint – for preparing for the task at hand, good leaders want to ensure they are supplying the right systems and processes to help their people achieve success, rather than restraining their strengths and preventing them from succeeding. Policemen, nurses, and businesspeople see their uniforms and business suits as support in readying their minds and bodies for work, just as harnesses help draft horses prepare for work. Similarly, the systems and processes available to team members must be regarded as helpful supports, so people are ready, willing, and able to make productive contributions.

If you visit a fitness center, you may find the weight machines, with their prescribed angles and measures, provide more support than free weights, so long as you know how to use them. In the workplace, people find procedures and processes provide more support than no tools at all, so long as they are effectively trained to use them. This discussion is not specifically about the harness, the weight machines, or the procedures and processes. These can all be useful tools and means to desired ends, which may include getting the ground plowed, the muscles taut, and the business profitable. When they recognize the means are providing support instead of throwing up unnecessary hindrances, individuals can reach their goals better and faster. Supportive constraints often prove more valuable than absolute freedom does.

CHAPTER 7

WE GET WHAT WE FOCUS ON

If you help your horse delight in what it can do, your horse will focus more often on what it can do.

I f you help your horse delight in what it can do, your horse will focus more often on what it can do. When a cowboy emphasizes, affirms, or encourages a horse's strengths or successes, the horse will tend to focus on that strength or success. This process works the same way with people: the more people focus on strength, the more they acquire strength and success. However, the opposite is also true. The more people focus on weakness, the more they acquire weakness. Therefore, good leaders want to recognize, emphasize, and appreciate strengths and successes, no matter how small.

The more you define a detailed picture of what you want, the more likely you'll receive just that. This principle is significant in horse training, sports, and business. Many meaningful stories involve athletes and their focus on a vision. In each story, the athletes envision the outcome they want (hitting a home run, making the perfect dive) and the correct attitudes, steps, and skills involved in achieving this outcome. They also envision performing these attitudes, steps, and skills perfectly. "See it happen" is a frequent mantra among athletes. By focusing on a vision of success, athletes program the subconscious part of their brain to implement winning attitudes, steps, and skills instinctively.

In many sports, athletes don't have time to consciously consider what they are doing moment by moment. For example, usually, when you're facing the pitcher, bat raised at the plate, there's not time to consciously work your way through the steps of hitting a home run. The time it takes for the ball to travel from the pitcher's hand to the home plate is less than the conscious brain's reaction time. So, the batter's subconscious brain must lead him or her through swinging the bat with timing and accuracy. Similarly, a diver doesn't have time to work through the steps of the perfect dive between leaving the board and hitting the water. Yet, some divers can and do achieve near-perfect dives.

Like these athletes, you too can achieve the visions you focus on through repetition, practice, and imagination. That is, you can practice both physically and mentally. Practice is a powerful form of focus. Many workplace activities require people to build experience through continuous practice. For example, in emergency drills and exercises, people practice the attitudes, steps, and skills needed for successfully responding to potential emergencies both individually and as a team. The phases of emergency management are preparedness, planning, response, and recovery. By the time people get to response and recovery, they must have been effective in their focus during the preparedness and planning phases.

To more deeply consider the idea of having a picture in your mind, think back to the illustration that accompanies Chapter 2. That illustration reveals the relationship between leadership and vision. It's one thing to have a vision and another thing to focus on that vision.

In *Natural Horse*Man*Ship*, Pat Parelli outlines a human's responsibilities in dealing with horses and emphasizes the importance of focusing on a shared vision:

> Use the natural power of focus. The human should come to understand and use the natural power of focus. What does focus mean? In every endeavor, sport, or anything we do, whether you're flying an airplane, driving a car, running a hurdle race, or snow skiing, focus and the line of direction are the most important ingredients. What does this mean in relationship to horses? If you look where you're going, your horse will take you where you want to go.

While many people have a vision for their lives or work, most don't effectively focus on those visions. If you focus on your vision, it is much more likely to come true. That's powerful. So, remember: having a vision is important, but focusing on the vision is crucial. Let your focus "take you where you want to go."

How does this happen? Focus on the vision by asking yourself a vision question: "Is what I'm about to do, say, or decide going to move me closer to or farther away from my vision?" If the answer is "closer," then obviously you should do, say, or decide that thing. If the answer is "farther," then don't. As a result, once you've answered the question, you move toward fulfilling your vision.

To emphasize this point further, we'll now discuss several different focus perspectives. While each perspective on focus appreciates the concept of *focus* to be elemental, each has a slightly different focus (no pun intended).

Heisenberg's uncertainty principle (applied in the physics field) says we get what we focus on. Specifically, according to the uncertainty principle, if we focus on a subatomic particle as energy, the particle will be energy; if we focus on the same particle as mass, the particle will be mass. You might think, in truth, the particle appears to be mass, or that I perceive the particle to be energy. Both of us may be right. As difficult as it is to believe or understand, the uncertainty principle says the particle is mass or energy – not both simultaneously – depending on how we apply our focus. This is one reason why we choose to focus on strengths, not weaknesses, in solution-focused leadership.

In each of the theories we discuss in *Taking the Reins* – Stephen Covey's notion that we affect other people's views of themselves, Heisenberg's uncertainty principle, and psychology's Pygmalion and Galatea effects (discussed below) – the premise that people get what they focus on is reinforced. According to the Copenhagen interpretation of the uncertainty principle, we learn the observer becomes part of the observed system. The idea that people get what they focus on – and that you can influence another person simply by what you focus on and how you focus – is significant in choosing whether people engage in helpful or harmful interactions with others.

Natural horse trainer Louis Wood directly affirms the importance of focus, saying, "If I make him [a horse] feel bad about what he can't do, he'll focus on what he can't do." Focus is crucial. Yet good leaders want to place the right focus on the right things for the right reasons. For a vision to be successfully transformed into reality, you must attend to two things. First, recognize what your subordinates (or your horse) are focusing on. Second, ensure what you're collectively focusing on is what you really want.

You need to recognize when your subordinates – or your horse – lose focus or focus on the wrong things. Returning to the ranch context, if a horse loses focus, a cowboy can lightly slap his own leg (or the horse's neck) to gain the horse's attention. At that point, the horse will instinctively pick up on what the cowboy is focusing on. The cowboy's slap shouldn't cause either party pain. Instead, its objective is to make a nonthreatening, sharp sound and grab the horse's attention. In the workplace, there are ways you can metaphorically slap your leg and gain subordinates' attention. Ask yourself, "What can I say, do, or emphasize so my people will respond (similar to what the horse did when it heard a slap), and refocus on the vision and task at hand?"

Returning to the horse and cowboy, a cowboy can focus on what his horse does well and on favorable experiences the two have shared. As a result, the horse will tend to continue to do well in the same ways and this shared focus will likely lead to additional, similarly favorable experiences. Jay Brewer, another natural horse trainer, takes a slightly different stance from Wood's on maintaining focus. He explains, "We must focus squarely. When I'm thinking of other things, I can't focus, the horse will know, and the work won't go well.

The horse won't learn." In the workplace, leaders can't expect others to focus if they don't focus. Leaders have to focus squarely: straight on, not tangentially. When leaders are distracted, those around them will recognize the loss of focus, and subordinates will either be distracted or think the leaders' requests are unimportant.

Another way of understanding focus is by remembering that you get what you measure. That statement's powerful corollary, you *don't* get what you *don't* measure, also applies. Therefore, because you may not be able to measure everything you think is worth measuring, what you choose to measure is significant. Remember, according to the Copenhagen interpretation of the uncertainty principle, an observer becomes part of the observed reality simply by measuring it.

In *Clinton Anderson's Lessons Well Learned*, Clinton Anderson states a similar lesson, "Take everything step-by-step." He elaborates, "Frustration, obstacles, and challenges in horse training – and in life – are best overcome by staying focused, finding balance, and taking things one step at a time." How can you transfer this practice to the workplace? As an example, think about a team member or a coworker. What are that person's strengths and weaknesses? Most people tend to focus on weaknesses, especially when those weaknesses could negatively affect what the team is trying to accomplish. However, as Stephen Covey argues, each person has his or her own paradigm, or filter, through which he or she deals with the world. Covey explains that how you perceive, or observe, a person both changes that person and how you relate to him or her. In short, all of us have significant influence on others' attitudes and behaviors. When people are busy exercising their strengths, they don't have the time or inclination to exercise their weaknesses. So, in your leadership role(s), focus on others' strengths.

Consider another set of powerful, psychological principles affecting those you work and live with. From psychology we've learned about the Pygmalion effect and the Galatea effect. The Pygmalion effect means people tend to meet the expectations others have of them, while the Galatea effect means people tend to meet the expectations they have of themselves. How can we apply this to good business practices? Well, when we focus on a person's strength, we expect that strength. If we have strengths in mind when we design a system, implement a practice or process, or think of people, we're creating the expectation of strengths in our designs, implementations, or thoughts. Subsequently, we're bound to get strength from the final product.

Yet, if we have weaknesses in mind when we design a system, implement a process, or think of a person, we create the expectation of weaknesses. Subsequently, we're bound to get weakness in the final product. At first, it seems as if people would never admit to designing a system or implementing a process around human weaknesses. However, consider the idea of "designing a foolproof system or implementing a foolproof process." By focusing on making something "foolproof," you're focusing on eliminating the possibility of a weakness appearing. The more important point is that you're focusing on weakness.

Let's be clear. We didn't say you should *ignore* a weakness or failure; instead, we said you shouldn't *focus* on a weakness or failure. A person can't fix a weakness or failure through more weakness or failure. The only way to fix a weakness or failure is through the use of strength. Therefore, as a leader you can recognize or address weakness or failure, but you should focus on strength and success.

HORSE SENSE

*The only way to fix a weakness or failure is
through the use of strength.*

Some large animals, such as cows and horses, will go up a flight of steps but will not go down. The steps are the same; the difference is fear. These animals won't go down steps because they fear the experience. In the illustration shown below, the horse is stuck; it's blinded by fear. The animal focuses on its fear and is stuck. The horse could go down the steps if given the proper encouragement and support, though. Natural horse trainer Jay Brewer says, "I can get Chip [a favorite horse] to go down steps if I have 10–15 minutes with him. I'll give him support, leadership, and confidence, and he'll trust me not to ask for anything that would hurt him."

To emphasize his point further, Jay gives the example of horses considering the action of crossing a cattle guard. A cattle guard is something farmers and ranchers build to save time and effort in opening and closing swinging gates. It's a series of about twenty parallel pipes (or small I-beams) embedded a few inches apart across a road, placed there instead of a gate (for example, as part of a road through a fence). Horses don't see this arrangement of pipes as a human would; instead, the arrangement creates an uncomfortable illusion for them. The horses focus on the possibility of injury, are instinctively frightened, and won't step on any part of the cattle guard. Therefore, they won't pass through the fence. When Chip and Jay are riding together, Chip would most likely focus on his trust of Jay and attempt to cross through the fence. However, the chances for Chip to get injured by stepping on parallel pipes a few inches apart are too high. Therefore, Jay has to be careful not to ask Chip to step on the cattle guard pipes. The lesson here is to get horses (and people) to focus on their strengths and the helpful attitudes of those they work with. The other lesson is gaining trust comes with responsibility: don't abuse the trust an individual has in you.

So, if you are focusing on strengths, when should you recognize and address others' weaknesses or failures? First, when an exhibited weakness or failure affects your or others' work, you should immediately identify the problem (that is, the complaint, not the cause) and the consequences. Then, you should indicate the steps needed to circumvent the weakness or failure so it won't recur. Second, when you're in a mentorship role and discussing a development plan, you should indicate the areas in which training and development will help a person be more effective.

Outside such situations, you should be recognizing and addressing strengths and successes. Good leaders should immediately indicate the contributions and the helpful consequences anyone makes. Remember, leaders improve weakness through focusing on strengths, not on weaknesses. Therefore, be vigilant to identify and respond to any strength or success, no matter how small. When a horse or a person shows competence and that competence is recognized or affirmed, the horse or person gains confidence. With more confidence, competence grows, and that growth inspires greater confidence. This cycle reinforces itself.

In this chapter, we also want to discuss improving strengths (first, by recognizing the strengths as valuable and, therefore, as worth improving) in situations in which people would benefit from training and development.

To this day, Harold remembers his high school art teacher saying he, Harold, was terrible at art. Harold's mother always said he couldn't sing; to this day, Harold doesn't try to sing, and maybe that's too bad. However, he has always loved art. Yet, for most of his life, he believed he couldn't *do* art because of what his high-school art teacher had said. After all, his art teacher should know best, right? Well, maybe not.

When he was in his fifties, Harold went on sabbatical and decided to try a local oil-painting class. Harold thought maybe he could just follow the process by using proper mechanics and his art wouldn't be so bad. So, he asked the art teacher, "Is it possible to teach someone who has no talent the mechanics of doing a decent job on a painting?"

The art teacher said, "Of course."

The rest is history: Harold has created a number of oil landscapes. Here's a painting Harold and Dave McCardle did together as collaborative artists:

Encouragement helped Harold focus on improving technical competence in artistic pursuits. Harold discovered his artistic strengths along the way.

Unfortunately, Harold missed out on forty years of knowing the joy of painting because of what someone said. He had almost never tried painting again after hearing that remark in high school. As a leader, you don't ever want to do to others what Harold's high school art teacher did to him. You want to help another person improve his or her favorable skills and attitudes. Often, good leaders help others by recognizing areas for improvement. They don't help by emphasizing weakness or contributing to bad feelings about what people think they can't do. The point wasn't to judge the quality of Harold's art. The point was to build Harold's confidence and enjoyment in doing art. In other words, this approach offers another way of revealing someone's hidden strengths.

So, in considering Harold's painting, we can ask, which art teacher was right, the high school art teacher or the evening-class art teacher? The painting depicts a beautiful scene, but from a technical standpoint its creation may align more with an engineering drawing than with modern art. Some art teachers might find this painting poor, while others might see it as good art.

The bottom line is this: by focusing on improving ourselves (personal mastery) and by focusing on others in appropriate ways, we, as humans and leaders, influence our experiences, others' experiences, and the work team's experiences in a favorable way. By choosing to focus on strengths, we're also choosing favorable outcomes and choosing to strive for excellence. By recognizing and focusing on other people's strengths, we encourage them to strive for excellence along with us. Since we get what we focus on, we'll achieve excellence together.

CHAPTER 8

ENCOURAGEMENT MAKES THE DIFFERENCE

Gain the horse's trust
through encouragement.

G ain the horse's trust through encouragement. Encouragement leads to the expectation of hope and possibility, higher self-esteem, a sense of security, personal strength, self-confidence, increased zest, and more courage. We believe *acts* of encouragement will increase *feelings* of encouragement (such as hope, possibility, security, and strength) and decrease feelings of discouragement or intimidation. Feelings of security lead to trust.

People, like horses, seek reassurance when they feel vulnerable. People experience vulnerability in a variety of settings but perhaps most often when they take a perceived risk, such as one of the following:

- attempting something new, unfamiliar, or particularly difficult;
- investing significant time and effort in a task; or
- changing something about themselves or their lives.

Reassurance is typically helpful and appreciated when behaviors, attitudes, self-confidence, and optimism are reinforced. Therefore, it's important to provide people with encouragement during difficult tasks and times of change. In the story that began Part I of this book, Tim and his grandpa encouraged their mounts on their way down the steep mountain by caressing the horses' necks and staying low. Those actions provided the horses with security, strength, and confidence.

The cowboy in the previous illustration is speaking words of encouragement to his horse. The horse is responding with comfortable confidence and eagerness to get on with the task. Though the horse doesn't interpret the precise meaning of the cowboy's words, it does interpret the meaning of the cowboy's voice, tone, and body language. We suspect the cowboy's tone of voice communicates appreciation, affirmation, and affection. It's easy to derive encouragement from that message.

For the purposes of this book, we think of encouragement in the following contexts:

- Encouragement is the process of facilitating the development of inner resources and confidence, bringing positive action.
- Encouragement is also the act of inspiring others. Giving encouragement shifts the focus from fear of change to recognizing and accepting opportunities in life.
- Encouragement is a motivation method that leads to a number of worthy results, including determination to make an extra effort, improved self-esteem, higher hope, and greater motivation.
- Finally, encouragement (and rewards) can provide someone with the impetus to move to a new position of enhanced relationships, leading to greater collaboration and performance.

When you encourage someone, you express your appreciation of and affirm the other person. Affirmation is more powerful than appreciation. Appreciation recognizes and supports what the other person does. Affirmation recognizes and supports who the other person is, celebrating that individual's character and strengths. Unfortunately, though, both encouragement and affirmation are rare. Yet using encouragement is a large part of teaching and preparing others. Professionals are responsible for helping to prepare the next generation to face and successfully navigate unseen challenges. Affirming a person's strengths is a fundamental part of good leadership.

HORSE SENSE

*Affirming a person's strengths is a fundamental part
of good leadership.*

Once people encounter discouragement and allow pressure to build without providing release, fear, anger, hurt, sadness, and more profound unhelpful feelings become much more likely. It makes sense to offer encouragement before encountering discouragement; it's the surest way to proceed. After all, the best way to resolve a problem is to prevent that problem in the first place. Then, the leader and the team don't have to solve the problem because the problem won't exist. Through encouragement, good leaders can create a place where discouragement doesn't exist or, at least, doesn't matter as much.

Most people would rather have hope than deal with fear or despair. By helping to develop courage in others through acts of encouragement, good leaders tip the balance away from despair and toward hope. Ultimately, acts of encouragement lead others to embrace change and be motivated to act. Encouragement enables creativity, productivity, and effectiveness, and the combination of these traits leads to improved performance. In addition, by acting in the best interests of others, leaders often become personally fulfilled and have positive feelings about themselves.

Given that acts of encouragement involve supporting, affirming, and inspiring others, how can you encourage someone, specifi-cally? You can encourage someone mostly through communication: by listening (especially reflection), asking open questions around strengths, and offering appreciation and affirmation. The most important skill any of us will learn in life is reflection, which is a listening skill (as discussed in Chapter 3). When you reflect, you demonstrate your active presence in the discussion and that the other participant (or participants) in the discussion matters. Reflection is encouraging and aids in creating a feeling of empowerment in the person you're speaking with. In solution-focused leadership, we lead through others' strengths. We use the skills of recognizing, encouraging, and affirming others' strengths. This focus on strengths encourages others to develop the confidence and courage to use their strengths, which, in turn, leads them to feel able to make a difference.

We believe encouraging someone is more helpful than simply responding to discouragement. Encouragement can and should be proactive, not reactive. No matter how confident, capable, mature, or successful people are, they will be helped by encouragement. Encouragement implies you believe in the other person and he or she matters to you. Thus, encouragement should nurture what is good, not bad.

Who needs encouragement? Each one of us. That's because we human beings are fragile. (We discuss the idea of fragile human beings in Chapter 22.) The best way to deal with fragility is through acts of encouragement. In developing good communication skills, good leaders learn to read facial expressions, body language, and tone of voice. Learn to look below the surface, so you can discern those times when someone most needs encouragement.

Here's one example of what encouragement looks and sounds like. Harold has a personal trainer who leads his workouts three times a week. The trainer continuously changes the exercises he encourages Harold to do. Often, the trainer includes activities Harold would rather not do because the exercises look difficult or painful. Yet Harold does them. Typically, after Harold has repeated the exercise several times, his trainer will say, "Two more," "You can do it," or simply, "Push!" Harold does what the trainer says for two reasons: first, the trainer should know how far Harold can go; and second, the trainer *believes* Harold can do it. The trainer never says, "You seem to be struggling," "This will be hard for you," or, "Maybe you'll do better next time." He always offers positive encouragement.

We all slip up or fail from time to time. A good encourager shouldn't seem to be affected by this. Instead, the encourager trusts we'll work at what we're doing and eventually be successful. He or she expresses belief by encouraging us to keep working and pushing ourselves in spite of our anxiety or fear. We're inspired to believe in ourselves because the encourager tells us, in words and actions, he or she believes in us.

So, what do encouragers do?

- First, encouragers make sure you know you matter to them.
- Second, they make sure you know how much they care about you, who you are, your work, your challenges and difficulties, and your hopes and dreams.
- Third, encouragers affirm you, not just in what you do and how well you're doing but also in who you are and what's special about you.
- Fourth, they appreciate you and what you contribute. They might even thank you for coming to work.

In one of their Solution-Focused Leadership program workshops, Harold and Tim worked with a physician. At the beginning of the workshop, the physician acted as many busy and important people do. (He was important in the hospital where he worked and the community in which he lived.) He was always in a hurry and didn't have time to show appreciation. One day, he decided he would make the effort to approach the people he worked with, including other physicians, nurses, nursing assistants, and custodians, to show his appreciation. He went up to them and thanked them for coming to work and contributing to the patients' welfare. The people he approached were shocked and a little mistrusting until they realized he was genuine. The physician made a change for the better in a workplace where great effort, focus, and well-developed interpersonal skills are required.

To see encouragement in action, watch parents, teachers, or pastors who influence children, students, or congregants to be the best they can be. Select those who seem to do their jobs most effectively. You'll observe encouraging attitudes and skills. You can also think back on your own experience by answering the following questions:

- Who was an encourager in your life?
- What did he or she say or do to encourage you?
- Who was a discourager in your life?
- What did he or she say or do to discourage you?
- Have you experienced an encourager following up on a discourager?
- How did the encourager affect you after you had been discouraged?
- How do you encourage others?

As you think over these questions, note that encouraging others helps us to encourage ourselves.

Encouraging people also shows you have faith in them. What does it mean to believe in someone? First, having faith in someone is different from trusting someone. When you trust people, you have evidence of their actions to consider when dealing with their competence, commitment, intent, and contributions. When you have faith in people, you go out on a limb because you have no specific action to base the belief upon. You expect them to contribute to and support an effort because you believe in the values and character they exhibit. You aren't able to rely on previous experiences that proved their competence, commitment, intent, or contributions. When you believe people and have faith they will do their best, you provide encouragement for them to do their best.

Finally, can you give someone too much encouragement? Actually, yes. When people respond to your encouragement with effort and confidence, give them a bit of space to show they can be successful on their own. As Pat Parelli writes, "'Don't encourage a horse who's already trying.' I mean, don't keep stimulating him after he's already responded with a slight try." Pat goes on to say that by overdoing the encouragement, people can overdo a good thing. However, most people will easily forgive you if they believe you're being genuine in your encouragement. If you can establish an environment in which your people feel comfortable telling you when enough is enough, you're probably on the right track.

PART I

STRENGTHS AT A GLANCE

PREFACE

1. Management is decision making; therefore, good management is good decision making.

2. When you supervise, you play the role of managing resources, most notably financial and human resources.

3. Leadership is recognizing, affirming, encouraging, and gathering others' strengths so the team can move toward a mutual vision.

4. A leader's decisions include those related to identifying problems, determining and achieving visions, and managing culture.

5. If you focus on fixing weaknesses, you're dealing with damage control. Yet if you focus on increasing strengths, you're striving for excellence.

CHAPTER 1:
LEADERS SURRENDER
TO OTHERS' *STRENGTHS*

6. When you give people time, space, and trust, their strengths rise to the surface.

7. A solution-focused leader recognizes, encourages, affirms, and harnesses others' strengths, while moving the team toward a mutual vision.

8. A solution-focused leader surrenders to others' strengths.

9. When you surrender to others' strengths, strengths you never knew about often appear.

10. You and your organization contribute, succeed, and make a difference by delivering excellence through strengths.

11. Solution-focused leaders are always on the lookout for moments when those around them do something well.

CHAPTER 2:
PEOPLE NATURALLY SEEK LEADERSHIP

12. True leadership is other-focused.

13. People prefer to work harder at their own ideas.

14. You lead by developing vision and encouraging people to contribute to that vision.

15. Leadership (and life) is about loving and learning with curiosity.

16. True leadership begins by gaining personal mastery through self-assessment, self-discipline, and self-management.

CHAPTER 3:
START THE RELATIONSHIP
BY SPENDING TIME LISTENING

17. Listening places you in the power and leadership position.

18. The most important skill you'll ever learn in life and work is reflection.

19. Reflection honors the other person.

20. Reflection helps the other person clarify his or her own thoughts and feelings.

21. A leader makes people feel encouraged and empowered.

CHAPTER 4:
UNDERSTANDING COMES BEFORE CONTROL

22. Those you supervise usually know the work process more intimately; sometimes, they know the client and their coworkers better than you do.

23. When your performance and destiny depend on others, your desire to control can get in your way. To surrender to others' strengths, a leader must put aside his or her desire for personal control.

24. Control tactics and fear may get you your short-term results; but, if you want long-term productivity and success, it's better to try trust and mutual respect.

25. Replace control with encouragement.

26. Expecting a person to be at a different place from where he or she actually is gets you nowhere.

27. If you outstrip the person you need to have alongside you, you'll be dealing with the gap between the two of you instead of with being productive.

28. Align your expectations with reality.

29. Communicate expectations, but don't expect people to be what or where they aren't.

30. Focus on those you work with so you know who and where they are. Then you can enlist them to join you in a spirit of collaboration, contribution, and productivity.

31. You need to understand your people; you also need to communicate your vision and expectations so your people understand what's needed.

CHAPTER 5:
PEOPLE'S STRENGTHS DIRECTLY REFLECT THEIR UNIQUENESS

32. A leader helps people want to make a desired change and will work toward creating what will benefit those people and the situation.

33. Recognize your team members' different strengths, resources, personalities, ways of perceiving the world, and ways of processing and acting on those perceptions.

34. People change themselves if you get out of their way.

35. A reward can be approval, affirmation, or acknowledgment.

CHAPTER 6:
A LEADER HARNESSES OTHERS' STRENGTHS

36. A leader relies first on building the right kind of relationship with those being led. A good relationship is the foundation from which favorable outcomes emerge.

37. People work best and most productively when their hearts are in the work.

38. When people recognize tools and techniques as supports and not restraints, teams can reach their goals better and faster than they can with absolute freedom.

CHAPTER 7:
WE GET WHAT WE FOCUS ON

39. Recall and use the vision question: ask yourself, "Is what I'm about to do, say, or decide going to move me closer to my vision or farther from it?"
    A. If the answer is "closer," do, say, or decide that.
    B. If the answer is "farther," don't.
    In this way, your vision comes true.

40. You get what you focus on, so focus on strengths.

41. You get what you measure, so be sure to focus on what you really want.

42. You have significant influence on others' attitudes and behaviors.

43. You live up to both what others expect of you and what you expect of yourself.

44. The only way to fix a weakness or failure is through the use of strengths or success.

45. Be vigilant to identify and respond to any strength or success, no matter how small.

46. Remember that with more confidence, competence grows; therefore, confidence grows, which supports greater competence. It's a virtuous, reinforcing cycle.

CHAPTER 8:
ENCOURAGEMENT MAKES THE DIFFERENCE

47. *Acts* of encouragement will increase *feelings* of encouragement (such as hope, possibility, security, and strength) and decrease feelings of discouragement or intimidation.

48. When you encourage, you express your appreciation for and affirm the other person.

49. Acts of encouragement involve supporting, affirming, and inspiring others.

50. Each one of us needs encouragement.

51. An encourager believes in you, so you'll work at what you're doing and be successful.

52. Encouragers first make sure you know you matter to them.

PART II

WE SUPERVISE THROUGH ANTICIPATING, SETTING, AND MEETING *EXPECTATIONS*

INTRODUCTION

TALMAGE AND APACHE: A DEVELOPING PARTNERSHIP

TIM THAYNE: As the white Dodge truck and its attached, red horse trailer drove away from my home, I couldn't help feeling a little sad. Yet, at the same time, I also felt vaguely relieved. I knew I was a whole lot smarter because of what was inside the trailer. Overall, I was unsettled to find myself with such mixed feelings.

Inside the trailer, being carried away to a new home, was a spirited gelding that had taught my son, Talmage, more about leadership, assertiveness, and the kind of girl you don't want to marry than any other individual could have. Through living and working with the horse, Talmage and I had learned a great deal about setting and meeting expectations, both my own and those of Talmage and my family, while coming to love, respect, and appreciate the horse, despite its difficult demeanor and poor upbringing.

This story had begun more than two years earlier when I flew to Billings, Montana, with my good friend, seasoned horseman Lee Caldwell. We were on our way to one of the largest horse auctions in the country. I was on a mission to bring home a couple of young horses for my two sons, Mitchell and Talmage. While on the plane, Lee gave me some expert advice: "Be careful not to get caught up in the moment. Don't start bidding when a great-looking horse comes into the ring if you haven't seen the horse out back in the corrals first." He explained how dishonest people sometimes drug a horse before it comes into the sales barn to make it seem calm and docile. As it happened, I was in the market for a calm, docile horse for my younger son, Talmage, who had little experience with riding.

By the end of the first day, although there were still 300–400 horses still to be sold, the skilled auctioneer had me believing every young horse coming through might be the last one available. I was ready to give up when out stepped *the horse*. I knew at first sight that I just had to have this one. Clearly this horse, a nice-looking gelding being ridden by a boy about Talmage's age, was special. The horse, a Gypsy Vanner, stood about thirteen hands tall and had a stocky build. As the young rider confidently rode him around the ring, the horse's long, beautiful mane and tail bounced. The animal completely enticed me. Before I knew it, I was bidding against another father who undoubtedly felt the same urgency to get that horse. Both of us ended up regretting the outcome: he regretted not getting this horse and I regretted paying as much as I had for it. The next day I purchased a second horse with more get-up-and-go for Mitchell, and then Lee and I returned home.

A week later, bundled up against the cold of an early March evening, my family gathered to watch our horses emerge from the trailer that had delivered them to our home in Utah. I had already shown the boys pictures of their horses. True to Talmage's character, my younger son had already bonded with the animal through the picture. He couldn't wait to be on the back of the calm, docile gelding I had bought especially for him. Talmage had already named his horse Apache. He expected Apache to have both the good looks from the photograph and the disposition I had described, based on my experience at the horse auction.

When Apache came out of the trailer, it took my brain a few seconds to register him. Was this the same horse I'd purchased the week prior? Something was radically different. This horse had the same markings and body type as the horse I'd bought. Yet, rather than showing a sweet and calm disposition, this horse pranced out of the trailer, defiantly shaking and holding his head. He pawed fiercely at the ground, oozing with attitude and energy. Lee's unheeded council on the plane stung my memory. I had been duped.

My mind raced as I tried to find a solution. Maybe I could get my two sons to trade horses. Talmage, with his inexperience and his calm and patient disposition, needed a gentle horse. Mitch was older, stronger, bigger, and more assertive, so he would be a better fit for Apache. Unfortunately, it was too late. Talmage wanted the special horse he had been dreaming about. There was no going back. Talmage had already given his heart to Apache.

As it turned out, Apache had been spoiled by his previous owner and was what people call "barn sour," which means Apache didn't like to be away from home or far from the other horses. So, when taken out for a ride, Apache would turn and fight to get back where he wanted to be as soon as he could. Thus began two years of rides in which, in the beginning, it looked as if Apache were riding Talmage, not the other way around.

Luckily, Talmage's laid-back demeanor came in handy during our first difficult experience with Apache. We lived in the middle of a neighborhood that had no equestrian trails nearby. While there weren't many convenient places for our family to ride, we knew of a twenty-acre open field about a block away. I decided to take the boys and horses there to give both some exercise and experience in an area larger than our own back pasture.

Initially Talmage did a great job of keeping Apache trotting, turning, and reined in as we made our way around the field. After a while, feeling a little anxious and uptight about being on a horse, Talmage got down from the saddle for a minute to stretch his legs. When he got back in the saddle, unfortunately, Talmage made a big, though not unusual, mistake, one that many novice riders make. I had taught Talmage to keep the reins in hand whenever he was on his horse, but Talmage became lackadaisical. Instead of taking hold of the reins before hoisting himself back into the saddle, Talmage grabbed only the saddle horn for stability and left the reins lying across Apache's neck. As soon as Talmage swung his leg over the horse and settled into the saddle, Apache took off across the field. Perhaps he was heading back to the barn. While he concentrated on staying on Apache, Talmage had absolutely no control and no way of stopping the horse, which had begun galloping at a dead run. Apache was heading for the paved road at the other side of the field.

I spurred my own horse to achieve a similar dead run and tried to catch up, all the while yelling at Talmage to grab one of the reins and pull hard, which would force Apache to run in a big circle. However, Talmage was in survival mode, clinging with all his might to the saddle horn; he was clearly not in control of the horse. When they were halfway across the field, Talmage finally tried to grab the reins, which were nearly within reach. I shouted again, louder this time, for

Talmage to turn his horse. Something clicked for Talmage, and he suddenly regained his normal, calm demeanor. Once he'd regained a level head, he was able to grab a rein with one hand and cling to the saddle horn with the other hand. He pulled the rein hard to the left, pulling Apache's head down to the horse's shoulder. Apache, forced to slow, started turning in circles.

After the incident, Talmage was shaken and still a little scared but not angry. I was just relieved. Together, my son and I assessed the situation. Talmage had averted disaster. First, he had regained his composure enough to gain control rather than bailing and jumping off the horse (a potentially dangerous move in the best of circumstances). Second, the horse and rider hadn't reached the street. We wouldn't want a horse running full speed, in shoes, on blacktop. Passing motorists might have felt the same way.

While Talmage might have been calm at that point, I certainly wasn't. My parental instincts had kicked into high gear while I had been thinking about what could have happened. I got onto Apache and rode him in circles until we were both exhausted. I wanted to teach the horse that running to the barn wouldn't be as comfortable and secure as riding around the field would be. I also wanted to teach Talmage about the concept of gentle firmness and the importance of developing a relationship with his horse.

Over time, Talmage grew as a rider and was able to demonstrate leadership in riding Apache. Early on, my son learned to prevent the horse's natural tendency to throw his (Apache's) head up by holding the reins tight. In addition to being barn sour and wanting to throw his head up to fight against the bit, Apache continually crowded people and stepped on them if they weren't watching carefully. So, whenever Apache walked over to people in what they might think was a friendly way, the horse was actually behaving in an extremely dangerous manner. Over time, Talmage successfully taught Apache not to crowd the rider. Whenever Apache got too close, Talmage would pressure the horse by backing him up a few steps (something a horse like Apache would rather not do). When he sensed Apache was reaching his limit, Talmage would stop backing up the horse, giving it release.

Talmage's patience paid off and, as a result, Talmage and Apache made a good team. They even won a 4H competition in which they had to demonstrate Talmage's control over his horse by walking in circles.

When our family took fishing trips up the nearby mountain, we would call on Talmage and Apache to take the lead and have them move to the front of our caravan. Talmage was confident and excited because Apache was the only horse confident enough to cross rushing streams. Our group needed and appreciated a confident, capable leader.

On one particular trip, when we were hunting deer on horseback, Talmage's saddle slipped up Apache's neck. The result was comical. Talmage, rocking back and forth on the loose saddle, looked as if he were riding a camel. Though Talmage enjoyed the situation temporarily, as soon as they found good ground, he calmly brought Apache to a stop, got off, and resaddled the horse. This situation, which undoubtedly would have been problematic at the beginning of their rider-horse relationship, was not a problem for two reasons. First, Talmage had significantly improved his riding skills. Second, at the same time, he had developed a trusting partnership with Apache. I stood by and watched proudly.

Through his relationship with Apache, Talmage received firsthand knowledge of vital life lessons:

- how critical it is for a horse to know what the appropriate behavior is in a given circumstance;
- how to determine where the boundaries are; and
- how to bring about appropriate consequences when boundaries are overreached (as in the case of backing up an aggressive horse).

However, I had my own vision of the boundaries and consequences regarding Apache. Through it all, I knew if Apache couldn't learn enough to be safe, he'd have to go.

Even though Apache did learn to be safe enough, Talmage eventually outgrew the horse, both in size and in understanding. We all (people and horses) have strengths and limitations. For example, one of Apache's strengths was his confidence in crossing streams. However, as Talmage grew in his ability as a rider, Apache's limitations in size, character, and skill held him back from what Talmage wanted a horse to do. Apache was bred to be more of a workhorse, and Talmage eventually became ready to graduate to a racehorse or barrel horse. Ultimately, the time came for Apache to go. The horse had to leave, not because of Talmage's inability to ride an initially difficult horse, but because of Talmage's growth into a stronger rider. Talmage had grown beyond being a kid who just wanted to have a horse to ride and love.

Significantly, if I could have changed things in the beginning, I would have. If my son hadn't connected to Apache so instantly, I might have returned the horse immediately. As a result, I would have interrupted or lost an opportunity for Talmage to learn a necessary life skill: asserting himself and showing leadership. Consequently, rather than being the wrong horse, Apache turned out to be the perfect horse. Struggle is often the greatest teacher. Character grows the same way muscles do, under effort and strain.

As Apache's new owner pulled away, I wanted to feel relieved someone else would be dealing with the horse's defiant attitude. Yet it was no use. A myriad of memories of Apache and Talmage together swirled in my head. I remembered the fun times, the scary times, and, ultimately, the growth I had seen in my son as a result of his partnership with this animal. Apache had inserted himself into our family history and, most importantly, left an indelible impression on my son's character. I'm forever indebted to this animal.

While Talmage cried to see Apache go, my son and I both knew we had helped Apache achieve better circumstances. My son knew why both he and the horse needed to move on. He understood the importance of continuing to grow and develop. Talmage will always have fond memories of his experience with Apache. We both hope Apache will find a good home where his own growth and development will make him a better member of his new family.

Tim's story about Talmage and Apache has many lessons, which we'll discuss in the chapters noted in parentheses:

1. Everyone, the horse as well as the humans, failed to have clear expectations. Tim expected a quiet horse. He also expected horse sellers to be honest. Though forewarned, he was naïve about a horse auction's business environment. As a result, Tim had to make unexpected, additional efforts to teach Talmage how to lead Apache. In turn, Talmage expected his new horse to be a safe friend. Instead, he received a poten-

tially dangerous horse that required careful attention. As a result, Talmage needed to learn more about how to set expectations, as well as discover that his job was to set expectations. Finally, Apache expected to be able to hang out with his horse friends at the barn. He had to learn Talmage's – and Tim's – expectations. Thus, Tim, Talmage, and Apache all had to adjust their expectations and learn the importance of setting clear goals (Chapter 9).

2. Significantly, Tim and Apache didn't recognize clear boundaries. Tim failed to recognize the extent to which people will misrepresent a horse's demeanor through drugs in order to sell that horse. In essence, he inaccurately defined a boundary of human behavior through optimism. From a physical standpoint, the empty lot represented very unclear boundaries for Apache. When he was in the empty lot, Apache didn't know the field's boundaries, nor did he have an understanding of appropriate spatial boundaries to maintain around people, since he was prone to invading people's space. His single experience at the auction taught Tim about a new boundary of human behavior, while collective experiences over time taught Apache to have a better understanding of physical and human-related spatial boundaries (Chapter 9).

3. Every decision you make leads to unintended consequences (along with any intended consequences you have). When choosing between given alternatives, most people think of pros and cons, but they don't focus on unintended consequences. Yet, because we can't always anticipate every reaction to a decision, there are always unintended conse-

quences. The unintended consequences in this story included matching an overly active and independent-thinking horse with a calm son. Happily, this unintended consequence also resulted in more favorable unintended consequences, such as teaching Talmage important life lessons. Had Tim known Apache's true nature, do you think he would have made the same decision to purchase this horse for Talmage? What unintended consequences might have resulted from a decision to purchase a more docile horse (Chapter 10)?

4. Tim originally planned to buy a gentle horse for his young, laid-back son, Talmage, and for Talmage to develop good riding skills. Tim didn't intend or desire that either he or his son should develop skills to train a difficult horse. Instead, Tim simply wanted to be able to share pleasurable riding experiences with Talmage. The initial problem was not having a horse for Talmage to ride. Tim thought he had found a quick fix for this problem by buying what appeared to be the first appropriate horse he had seen. He brought the horse home and Talmage rode it. In the short term, the problem was solved.

In the longer term, Talmage had to develop skills to retrain a difficult horse, not to ride a gentle horse. Tim spent much of his energy on the taxing activity of training a difficult horse, thereby losing the opportunity to spend time on pleasurable family interactions. The lesson is to know what you're buying, to consider alternative choices more fully, and to recognize the intended and unintended consequences of your decision (Chapter 10).

5. When Apache crowded Talmage, Tim taught his son to put the horse in an uncomfortable situation (walking backward). Apache didn't like the consequences of violating Talmage's boundaries. After being repeatedly subjected to this consequence, Apache learned to avoid the dangerous behavior of crowding people. To correct this behavior, Talmage purposefully and consciously stressed the horse. However, whenever he sensed Apache was reaching the limit of reasonably endured stress, Talmage would stop backing up. This kind firmness gave Apache release from the stress of this awkward and uncomfortable situation and helped the horse understand his rider's expectations (Chapter 11).

6. Talmage received the unexpected challenge of working with a difficult horse. This challenge encouraged Talmage to change his thinking and to stop acting based on what was normally comfortable. As he exerted himself in new ways, Talmage was rewarded with the satisfaction of learning and of achieving success with his horse. These rewards encouraged Talmage to take additional risks with Apache. Who changed the most and changed in the most helpful ways, Talmage or Apache? During their time together, who learned the most (Chapter 11 and Chapter 15)?

7. When he had to regain control over Apache, Talmage instinctively took a soft, encouraging, and hopeful approach, instead of a hard, threatening, and fear-oriented approach. Not surprisingly, the soft approach worked, even on a headstrong animal like Apache (Chapter 12).

8. Because Talmage naturally surrenders to others' strengths, he did very well in surrendering to Apache's strengths. Talmage, a kind-hearted kid, always sees the strengths in others. However, he needed to learn more about how to set clear expectations. Setting expectations requires the firmness and strength to consistently demonstrate the consequences of either meeting or not meeting expectations. Talmage, who was much better at demonstrating softness than firmness, had to learn his job was to set expectations. Apache helped Talmage by revealing the need for clarity and firmness (Chapter 12).

9. When pulling on one rein to turn and prevent Apache from running back to the barn, Talmage caused a transition in his horse's direction and behavior. Fortunately, Talmage used the right amount of pressure on the rein. If Talmage had yanked the rein back as hard as possible, the horse could have flipped over entirely. When Talmage rode Apache in a series of circles, he was, in a sense, redirecting Apache's unwanted and problematic behavior and channeling it into behavior that could be controlled (Chapter 11 and Chapter 13).

10. When he got back on Apache that first day in the field, Talmage had lost focus and separated from the correct process he had learned for mounting a horse. Given the lack of focus, Apache wasn't confused (as a worker might be when violating the steps of a work process). Instead, Apache felt free to do whatever he wanted, process or no process (Chapter 14).

11. As Talmage increased his riding skills and learned the processes he needed to ride safely and well, Apache's bad habits (e.g., being barn sour, throwing his head up to fight against the bit, and crowding people) diminished. These improvements resulted in the ability of the rider-horse partnership to successfully complete the work tasks assigned to them. Talmage learned that he could prevent Apache from fighting the bit by keeping the reins tight (Chapter 14).

12. Tim and Talmage had to address Apache's crowding issue before Apache had an opportunity to really hurt someone. To control Apache, Talmage also needed to learn to think two steps ahead of what he was going to do with the horse. When he learned to hold the reins to prevent Apache from fighting the bit, Talmage was considering what would take place before something happened (Chapter 15).

13. Tim spent time and energy ensuring Talmage was safe. Simultaneously, he gave Talmage an opportunity to learn from Apache, despite the horse's limitations. When Talmage outgrew Apache, though, Tim had the wisdom to let the horse go to a place where his strengths would be better suited to a new owner's needs. In the meantime, Tim found a new horse for Talmage (Chapter 16).

14. Typically, novice horse riders would listen to their instructor and jerk the reins back to try to stop a runaway horse. At the same time, the riders' natural fear instinct would likely cause them to hold tight to the horse's midsection with their legs, a signal a horse would interpret as "go faster." Those

two instinctive actions send conflicting messages. In Talmage and Apache's case, the lack of clarity resulting from conflicting messages could have led to the horse's confusion and discomfort. Fortunately, Talmage was careful in pulling on the reins and didn't put increased pressure on the horse's midsection. As a result, Talmage sent Apache a clear message about what he wanted (Chapter 16).

15. A novice manager or supervisor's natural inclination is to take a back seat and not truly supervise or manage (that is, make decisions). We understand a rider should lead and a horse should follow. First, however, rider and horse need to get their rules straight and settle into a comfortable partnership. One central theme of the Talmage and Apache story is the value of maturity: as they worked out their partnership, Talmage and Apache each matured (Chapter 16).

In Your Workplace ...

The principles and practices illustrated through Talmage and Apache's story provide an engaging segue to Part II ("We Supervise through Anticipating, Setting, and Meeting *Expectations*"), in which we discuss the relationship between expectations, consequences, and effective supervision. We have organized the following chapters based upon a progression of thought:

- You communicate expectations clearly by setting boundaries and consequences (Chapter 9).
- You recognize each alternative for fixing a problem has

unintended consequences, so you identify which alternative includes unintended consequences you can live with. Often, determining a fundamental solution takes imagination and patience, since the fundamental solution usually requires delayed gratification. In other words, you can't allow yourself to get caught up in quick fixes (Chapter 10).

- You influence a person's attitude or behavior effectively by combining reassuring pressure with timely, comforting release from the pressure. This combination promotes an atmosphere of encouragement for building trust (Chapter 11).

- You choose the Theory Y approach to management in which you encourage people's innate desire to do their best (Chapter 12).

- You address the ever-present need for change by asking for and encouraging it while ensuring people know you care about the possible loss of their present comfort levels (Chapter 13).

- Your job is to help people move through the steps of an effective, efficient process designed to help them achieve success while doing their jobs (Chapter 14).

- You pay attention to details and listen carefully so you discover potential problems before they happen (Chapter 15).

- You provide clarity and comfort around what's expected and how to be successful by encouraging and supporting behavior that builds trust and accountability (Chapter 16).

CHAPTER 9
WE ALL NEED CLEAR
EXPECTATIONS AND BOUNDARIES

Horses need to be given clear expectations and boundaries, and be made aware of the consequences of failing to meet those expectations or of overreaching those boundaries.

Horses need to be given clear expectations and boundaries, and be made aware of the consequences of failing to meet those expectations or of overreaching those boundaries. Try to recall a situation in which you thought you did a great job, only to find out the expectations of your boss or the client weren't in sync with what you understood them to be. How did you feel? What did you do? Were there clear consequences? Now, try to recall a time when you received something from one of your team members that didn't meet your expectations. How did you feel? What did you do? Understanding your answers to all these questions will help you hone in on one significant aspect of successful supervision and leadership: setting and meeting clear boundaries and expectations.

Natural horse trainer Jay Brewer uses the example of working with a horse that is learning to perform a side pass to demonstrate the frustration that can result from unclear expectations. The side pass is an unusual and unnatural movement for a horse, but the horse needs to be adept in this movement so it can participate in moving sideways to help the cowboy perform tasks such as opening or closing a heavy gate while the cowboy is still in the saddle. In this instance, Jay wanted one of his favorite horses to make a side pass to the left. Because the horse didn't understand the maneuver, it didn't know what to do. Jay hadn't set expectations for the maneuver. In other words, he hadn't trained the horse properly for this task.

This example generates two issues: first, setting expectations; second, preparing the horse to understand those expectations. Since Jay happens to be right-handed, he didn't work the horse's left side as much as the right side. As a result, Jay hadn't prepared the horse to understand the rider's expectations for a side pass to the left. Consequently, when Jay needed his horse to side pass to the left, it balked.

The horse didn't know what to do because it didn't understand what Jay expected and it didn't know how to respond to Jay's signals. Frustrated, Jay got off the horse, shut the gate himself, and walked away, leaving the horse confused.

To the best of its ability, the horse had followed Jay. In Jay's words, "The horse didn't want to be difficult; the horse wanted to do well for me." As a result, Jay realized the horse wasn't defying him. The horse wanted to be with Jay, but it just didn't know what Jay expected. Because Jay didn't look ahead to future activities and therefore didn't adequately train the horse to make a side pass to the left, Jay had to make extra effort with that gate. Eventually, Jay had to get over his frustration so this rider-horse partnership could be productive in the rest of their daily tasks.

As in Talmage's challenge to supervise Apache, a horse that had little or no experience with expectations, Jay realized he needed to set clear expectations for his horse (in this case, to side pass to the left). Having never been instructed to do otherwise, Apache had learned he could do what he wanted, whenever he wanted. The horse experienced consequences for the first time when Tim rode him in circles instead of allowing him to run back to the barn. Through circling, Tim prepared Apache for an effective partnership with Talmage.

On horseback and in the workplace, clearly communicated expectations are fundamental to effective supervision and leadership. To be effective, we must meet the following needs:

- We need to determine exactly what we expect.
- We need to communicate our expectation(s) clearly.
- We need to ensure the other people have interpreted our expectation(s) exactly.

Visions are expectations, as are goals, objectives, and milestones. The crucial ingredients in high-performing organizations are clear expectations, clear boundaries, and a clear indication of the consequences when expectations aren't met or boundaries are overreached. Horses and humans both succeed when they know what's expected of them[3] (Chapter 7).

HORSE SENSE

Horses and humans succeed when they know what's expected of them.

Visions, goals, objectives, and milestones can all be used to communicate clear expectations. To be most effective, good leaders must focus on those expectations. These days, organizations are doing better than ever in stating formal expectations. However, by and large, they are doing a lousy job of focusing on those expectations. People (or organizations) focus on expectations when they test statements of intention, decisions, and actions against those expectations. For example, you focus on a goal when you say to team members, "This decision will move us closer to this goal because …" (To review the vision question and how it applies to this topic, see Chapter 7.)

Notice how tightly having a vision and communicating the vision (Chapter 2), focusing on the vision (Chapter 7), and meeting expectations (this chapter) are tied together. As we consider procedures for developing and using vision statements, we know the same

---

[3]Clinton Anderson describes a similar concept in *Clinton Anderson's Lessons Well Learned*: "To be effective, you have to be understood." He elaborates, "Black-and-white communication with horses creates the [type of] understanding that helps solve problems and paves the way for achieving your highest goals."

procedures and rules apply to goals, objectives, and milestones, since they're all expectations.

Expectations are everywhere, whether people like it or not. A client has a need; that's reality. A client has expectations around that need; those are abstractions. Because expectations are abstractions, the need and the expectations usually don't match up perfectly. The imperfect match between the client's need and the client's expectations may be the origin of the saying, "The client lies." While clients don't often intentionally lie, they may not recognize exactly what the need is or may not communicate either the need or the expectation clearly. In dealing with clients, a leader's job is to use communication skills (especially reflection, as discussed in Chapter 3) to draw out the expectation as perfectly as possible. A good leader knows clients ultimately expect their needs to be fulfilled.

Leaders can try to model clients' expectations (abstractions of the *need*) through requirement statements (abstractions of the *expectations*). Requirements define what people design, build, or deliver to meet the client's needs, as the client expresses his or her needs in the form of expectations. The process works like this:

1. The client begins with an undefined and unwritten need.
2. This need leads to the client's conscious or subconscious expectations.
3. These expectations are abstractions of the client's need.

So, to best meet the client's expectations, the client's often-contractual business requirements must be put in writing. Requirements are, in turn, abstractions of the expectations. (As Joseph Juran, a man of total quality management fame, says, "Quality is meeting requirements.")

As the people asked to design, build, and deliver a product or service to meet the requirements statement do their work, they develop specifications. Engineers, technicians, executives, and others want business and system requirements communicated as specifications. These specifications are abstractions of the *requirements* statements. With so many layers of abstraction, no wonder it's so difficult to fulfill the client's specific need.

In the workplace, everybody has expectations of others. Therefore, it's highly possible for any person who has expectations to experience a struggle in transmitting those expectations. The ability to recognize, faithfully interpret, communicate, affirm, and ultimately meet expectations represents a skill set that, once gained, will spell success for the individuals and organization alike. It's best to begin learning these skills through working on the day-in, day-out expectations people have of each other. We all need to practice communicating our expectations.

Beyond that, people need to practice asking for statements and clarifications of expectations. For example, you might say to a child, "I want you to clean your room." In this instance, you've set an expectation, albeit not very well. Try something more specific: "I want you to pick up your toys and put them in the toy box before you go out to play this morning. If you don't pick up your toys and put them in your toy box, you can't go out to play." Then you can say, "To make sure I communicated well, tell me what I asked you to do." At that point, if the child doesn't meet your expectation, he or she doesn't go out to play. That, in turn, creates another expectation.

People also need to have clear boundaries. Say each worker has a domain of responsibility in the workplace. Workers can consider all their duties within that domain of responsibility. To keep themselves out of trouble, they can delimit the domain by putting boundaries around it. Otherwise, they can wander into all kinds of trouble without knowing it. For example, when workers don't clearly understand their roles and responsibilities, they're in one kind of trouble. When they don't clearly understand the roles and responsibilities of those whose domains of responsibility bump into theirs, they're in a second kind of trouble. A third kind of trouble involves gaps in responsibility. In other words, when these gaps appear, things fall through the cracks. The fourth kind of trouble deals with overlapping responsibility: workers approach the same tasks from different directions and end up undoing each other's work. As a result, the decision or action last performed, even when not performed correctly, prevails.

Think back to the story about Apache. This horse wasn't unusual in his tendency to crowd his riders; horses have a tendency to crowd people, especially if they expect something, such as a treat. Because of its size, a horse can hurt a cowboy when their personal spaces converge. Tim taught Talmage to put Apache in an uncomfortable situation when the horse started crowding. Talmage disciplined his horse by walking Apache backward, which is something most horses dislike doing. As it turned out, Apache didn't like the consequences of violating Talmage's boundaries. These consequences influenced Apache and led him to stop his dangerous behavior of crowding people.

So, success can be defined as meeting expectations. In *Quality Is Free*, Philip Crosby also defines quality as conformity to requirements. According to Crosby, not only do people need to set expectations and boundaries, they also have to meet expectations and work within their boundary conditions. In your interactions with others, you must be clear in communicating the consequences of not meeting expectations and of overreaching boundaries.

People should always group together expectations, boundaries, and consequences. When Tim first purchased a horse for his naturally quiet and kind second son, he believed a maxim based on honesty: "What you see is what you get." Expecting he'd been presented with a fair and honest representation of the cute little Gypsy Vanner, Tim bought the horse on the spot. Unfortunately, Tim and his family ended up with a horse that had never learned clear boundaries or been presented with effective consequences for problematic behavior.

After the "perfect" horse was delivered to their home, Tim, Talmage, and the rest of their family learned an important lesson about expectations, boundaries, and potential (and realized) consequences. In his new home Apache didn't know the expectations that would be set by his new rider (his supervisor). As a result, Apache overstepped Talmage's boundaries and suffered the consequences. Eventually, though, Apache changed his own behavior. Overall, the most significant consequence for Tim and his family was having to live and work with a horse that was quite different from the one they had expected.

Each decision presents an expectation. However, unless supervisors follow through on their decisions with corresponding actions, there are no consequences for failing to meet expectations or for overreaching boundaries. For example, consider again the child being asked to clean a room. If a decision doesn't have a prescribed and planned corresponding action tied to it, that decision is counterproductive. In other words, if you don't know what action you're going to take to implement a decision, don't bother making that decision.

This is an important principle, since an action implemented represents a boundary and boundaries are limitations, restrictions, or rules. Making a decision presents an expectation about what action you want an individual to perform. If the horse or person doesn't know what action you intend to take in relation to your decision, that individual won't be motivated to produce the action and will be frustrated. Moreover, if the action isn't carried out within the boundaries, there must be consequences. Consequences ensure the decision, action, and corresponding boundaries are all real and meaningful.

This principle applies to a variety of scenarios. For example, Harold has spent most of his professional life designing and building management tools: information systems, organization structures, software packages, operations research models, policies, plans, procedures, culture tools, and so forth. The biggest lesson in all of his experience is *fit*. Each management tool must fit the domain of responsibility to which it belongs. Put another way, each tool must meet a clearly defined need (the ultimate expectation), no more, no less.

When Harold designs and builds management tools, he finds that clients often change what they want or recognize additional needs as they observe the management-tool project's progress. Developing a solution to fit a given need exactly is difficult enough. When the given need's design changes in mid-stream, you risk developing a solution that won't fit the new or changed need. After changing development activities to fit additional needs, the result may not even fit the original need. Thus, whenever project changes occur, regardless of where people are in the process, a reevaluation of the original needs statement must be completed and the needs statement formally rewritten, allowing for appropriate, further changes from the client.

We're sure you've had similar experiences in trying to meet ill-defined or changing expectations. Misunderstandings about expectations are part of the adventure of entrepreneurial enterprise. There are two keys to overcoming such misunderstandings: first, continually communicate your interpretation of the expectations as formally and clearly as possible; second, carefully and definitively determine the boundaries of the domain of responsibility you're serving. The listening skill of reflection (discussed in Chapter 3) is a wonderful strategy to use when ensuring you understand expectations. Recall what a parent can say to a child about cleaning up: "I want to be sure I've expressed myself clearly. Would you tell me what you heard me say?"

Finally, we want to emphasize the word *clear* in the principle stated at the beginning of this chapter: "Horses need to be given clear expectations and boundaries, and be made aware of the consequences of failing to meet those expectations or of overreaching those boundaries." Through clarity, you can recognize whether you understand your own needs. As we discuss in Chapter 16, through clarity, we successfully communicate our expectations so the other people can define a good requirement or a way to meet the expectation. Famed communication expert Rudolf Flesch says we can't think any more clearly than we can express ourselves. This statement is an argument for learning to write and speak clearly. Because what's clear to one person could very well not be clear to another, you have to verify others understand what you write or speak. Try saying, "I want to make sure I've expressed myself clearly. Please tell me what you heard me say."

CHAPTER 10

ALL ATTEMPTS TO MEET NEEDS OR FIX PROBLEMS RESULT IN UNINTENDED CONSEQUENCES

Think two steps ahead of your horse.

Think two steps ahead of your horse. You have an imagination; your horse doesn't. If you're a cowboy working with a horse, you – not the horse – are responsible for producing the vision of a proposed activity. Then, you are responsible for communicating the vision to your horse. You have the ability to imagine all the details associated with accomplishing the vision (how, what, when, where, and with whom). You are the one who understands consequences for multiple options long before any one action is attempted or completed. You can warn the horse or guide it away from trouble, if and when necessary, because you have the ability to recognize something's about to happen before that thing happens. In response, the horse contributes its natural instincts, as in the story of Tim and his grandpa on the mountain. The cowboy contributes imagination and decision making. Each uniquely contributes to the partnership in ways that make the partnership more effective.

HORSE SENSE

You have imagination; your horse doesn't.

When people are involved in completing a task or resolving a difficulty, as the process progresses they may try to anticipate ways to do a better job or address the difficulty more effectively. By taking a little time, you can determine a number of different ways to approach the task or determine ways to resolve the difficulty. An obvious question is: which way is best? Unfortunately, people typically don't ask the obvious questions, let alone consider a relatively complete set of alternatives.

Typically, people are in a hurry or are thinking beyond what they're dealing with at the moment. Imagination, which is a strength, also has the potential to get people into trouble. If you see a task to do or a problem to fix, you may come up with what looks like a reasonable idea, and then set off implementing the idea. Unfortunately, usually it's not best to implement the first idea you come up with. Sometimes, people do consider a few alternatives and take a few moments to identify pros and cons for each. However, for all of that forethought, most people don't usually consider unintended consequences for each alternative. That's a mistake. Unintended consequences can adversely affect someone else or, in fact, make the original problem worse.

Many of us have made matters worse through our well-intended efforts. For instance, Harold and his family once owned and operated a country inn. It's important for a country inn to have well-designed, well-implemented, and well-maintained grounds. The grounds at Harold's country inn included six acres of grass. One of Harold's contributions to the family's country inn was to mow the grass. In the early spring months, that task took about eight hours and had to be repeated every few days.

Given this description, you might think Harold's problem was spending too much time tending to the grass. In fact, Harold's problem was not spending enough time with his family. To make matters worse, the family was quite vocal about their perception of Harold prioritizing the grass over his own family. Harold couldn't convince everyone that if he didn't tend to the grass when it needed to be mowed, bigger problems would develop. Overgrown grass would clog the mower and mowing would consume even more effort and time while creating more frustration. Thus, spending less time on mowing before the grass overgrew would have an adverse impact on the business itself.

The problem of not having enough time for his family weighed on Harold's mind. One day, while driving home, Harold noticed wildflowers growing in the highway median. He immediately made the connection between lush, colorful wildflowers and the idea of a country inn. When he proposed the idea, his family agreed that it was a great idea to replace their grass, which needed mowing, with wildflowers, which didn't. So, the next spring, they planted wildflowers on about three acres of their grounds, replacing the grass. Because the wildflowers were lush and colorful and needed no mowing, the time invested in planting them was well spent. Harold wisely devoted his saved time to hanging out with his family, and everyone was pleased with the results – for a while.

When summer came, the weeds arrived, and tall, ugly milkweeds appeared in droves. Harold's family knew it wouldn't do to have tall, ugly weeds in the middle of the grounds of a beautiful country inn. Making matters worse, the milkweeds seemed to flourish more than the wildflowers did. To meet his responsibility of keeping the grounds in good shape, Harold turned his attention to pulling the weeds without trampling the wildflowers. The following year, the weeds seemed to be even hardier than the wildflowers. That spring, Harold ended up spending four hours a week mowing the remaining grass and about six hours a week dealing with the weeds. (Plus, he had to plant and replant the wildflowers.) Harold's good intentions to fix the situation ended up making his original problem worse.

We're sure you can think of times at work or at home when you made your best effort but ended up making things worse. Most likely you haven't thought about times when your best effort made problems for someone else. Finally, you've probably also had experiences in which so much time had elapsed between your fix and the worsening of your original problem that you didn't realize your fix was what made the original problem worse. These unintended consequences create dilemmas.

To resolve the difficulty of unintended consequences before you decide on a plan of action, take the time to identify a number of alternative solutions to a problem or alternative tasks to meet a need. When Harold first thought about planting wildflowers, the solution to his problem of mowing the grass seemed obvious. He felt no need to take the time to dream up alternative solutions. In contrast, after you have imagined several alternatives, work hard – you can use your imagination again – to define potential unintended consequences for each alternative. You'll find you can live with some unintended consequences, but you can't live with others. Now, you're powerful. You've accepted potential unintended consequences, so you won't be surprised when and if they occur.

What's more, you can make even more of an effort to identify what you feel is the fundamentally sound solution with few unin-tended consequences. You'll find implementing the fundamental solution will usually require delayed gratification on your part. In contrast, the allure of quick fixes will typically get you stuck in such a way that you'll end up not being able to implement the fundamental solution.

Talmage and Apache's story is full of unintended consequences. Tim and his family had to deal with Apache's problems, instead of simply supporting Talmage's enjoyment in riding a horse. However, not all unintended consequences are problematic. For example, discovering how to deal with a difficult horse yielded unintended benefits to Talmage in the form of learning and personal growth. In the end Tim's original plans for Talmage and his horse weren't implemented, while original expectations weren't met because the unintended consequences of a quick fix were too far-reaching. Over time, Tim overcame these unintended consequences by reevaluat-ing the situation and setting and meeting new goals. As with Tim's experience, unintended consequences can prompt your imagination to develop new, often better goals, and you can then evaluate your results against those new goals.

In business, we always strongly suggest you consider the unintended consequences for each alternative decision and action you can take when solving a problem. When people are presented with a need to do something or to resolve a problem, often their first instinct is to rapidly figure out a task that leads to a solution. In these cases, the solution is a quick fix that resolves the problem at hand in the short term. After a short-term resolution, people move on to the next issue or task. They forget about the solution they used to solve the previous problem. They don't think about and aren't aware of a few important issues.

For example, the solution could have generated a problem for another person who is close enough to be adversely affected by the solution's fallout. The solution could generate a bigger problem at a later time. Sometimes, the affected person isn't so close; sometimes, the later time is much later. The repercussions of a solution are often out of sight, out of mind. Later, when it's too late, people discover the unintended consequences. To prevent this, you can consider unintended consequences for each alternative decision and action in advance, and then choose the set with potential consequences you can best live with *before making the decision or taking the action.*

CHAPTER 11

WE RESPOND TO
ENCOURAGEMENT AND REWARDS

---

*Everything you do with your horse is
a form of pressure and release.*

Everything you do with your horse is a form of pressure and release. Think about a person you've unsuccessfully tried to influence in one of the following ways:

- You tried to change his or her thinking or behavior.
- You wanted the person to take a new approach to a task.
- You wanted him or her to accept a new set of responsibilities.

- You encouraged the person to initiate a more progressive or more aggressive set of business development activities.
- You hoped the person would move to approve your plan or adjust to new support systems.

Now, think back to your actions in that case, or others. Have you focused on applying pressure to help someone move to what you believe is a better solution? When you get any type of favorable response, do you apply more pressure to keep things moving? When you apply greater pressure, does the other person balk or dig in?

Think about a cowboy trying to move a balking, uncooperative horse from one side of a work area to another. When the cowboy pulls on the halter of a horse weighing a half-ton or more, he faces a task that will *only* yield success if the horse agrees to move. A human can be even more difficult than a horse. When you "pull" or "push" a person, figuratively speaking, you're applying pressure. Often, such pressure makes the person uncomfortable and, perhaps, insecure. This person may not be bigger or heavier than you are, but he or she can still resist in surprising ways. In your life you may have learned that movement is significant enough to be considered successful only when a person finally chooses to move. The meaningful question, in that case, is whether you've made the person's choice easier or more difficult.

Given steady and firm pressure on its halter, sooner or later a cowboy's horse experiences enough curiosity about what's going on to budge, just slightly, in the desired direction. If you watch closely while applying gentle pressure, the people you're eager to guide in a new direction will hesitantly soften their reticence and, maybe, even take a hesitant step forward. Like the cowboy, you may be tempted to respond to this slight response to your invitation for change with

even greater pressure. People often think they can gain momentum and get other people to change before they even realize what they've done. They hope to overcome reluctance with insistence.

Most of the time, acting on the temptation to apply greater pressure results in the adoption of a rigid, dug-in stance by the person who's being invited to change. Luckily, the caring cowboy is too smart to act on such a temptation with his horse. Instead, when the horse barely moves in the desired direction, the cowboy releases his pressure. The horse feels rewarded by the comfort of the relaxed pressure. This interaction brings the following message to the horse: if you move in the indicated direction, you'll receive comfort and security. You may not achieve complete comfort and security in the new, perhaps distressing position, but you'll achieve the comfort and security of diminished pressure.

As soon as the horse registers the comfort of release, the cowboy applies pressure again. This time, even if the cowboy's pressure is less, the horse responds more quickly and less reluctantly. Immediately, upon discerning the horse's response, the cowboy releases the pressure again, thereby rewarding the horse. After the entire effort, which only takes a few minutes, the horse starts following the cowboy around their work area, just like a faithful companion.

Discussing the difference between being assertive and aggressive in *Far Away Horses*, Buck Brannaman states, "This is the time to release, to back off, and allow the idea to take shape in the other person's, or the horse's, mind. It's the most important lesson in the art of conversation, no matter whom you're trying to communicate with. It's all about learning to keep your mouth shut, learning to listen and watch, [and] learning how to release and let go."

The combination of firm but reassuring pressure and rewarding and comforting release creates an encouraging atmosphere and a foundation for building trust. Encouragement and trust are powerful tools. In the workplace people often encounter situations in which they have difficulty with another worker regarding an issue. Perhaps the issue is a need for collaboration on a change in the work. Every time the issue of change arises, one person – either the person asking for change or the person being asked to make the change – doesn't compromise and increases the "stiff-leggedness" of the situation. In reviewing this situation, you might think, "Oh no! Here we go again." These two people are stuck in a difficult cycle of attitude and behavior. Situations like this can lead to rigidness and resistance. One significant way to reverse a difficult cycle of attitude and behavior between people is through the behavior and attitude associated with encouragement. (See Chapter 8 for a discussion of the importance of encouragement.)

What about your leadership? When you invite a person or a group to change position, you may be applying uncomfortable pressure. Learn not to overreact to the first, hesitant steps of the person or group moving in the desired direction. In addition, learn not to apply increased pressure with a sense of demand and urgency. Rather than demanding more of the person or group, try to respond – not react – to the first favorable step with release, or encouragement, and follow it with another invitation to move forward.

How much pressure should be applied? The answer is: the right amount. Natural horse trainer Louis Wood helps here by offering another principle: "You need to use enough pressure to encourage response. Not enough pressure shows indifference." (We'll discuss the issue of indifference in Chapter 24.) Your job, as a leader, is to encourage the people you're responsible for to move physically, mentally, emotionally, or socially toward the objectives you have set to improve the shared work. Yet, whether it's favorable or unfavorable, change often leads to stress, and many times stress leads to conflict. You can use encouragement to help lessen the stress involved in changing direction(s).

To venture out from a known position, people need encouragement and affirmation. However, you need to be careful not to apply too much or too little pressure, as either can be debilitating. Too much pressure implies dominance, while too little implies indifference. In turn, dominance implies you think you're more important than your coworkers, while indifference implies you don't care about the work or your coworkers. You can learn the right amount of pressure to apply through trial and error. The key is to be purposeful with the pressure, to pay close attention to the responsiveness of those you're pressuring, and to learn from what works and what doesn't. Each person and each situation is different. (We discuss the importance of recognizing each person's uniqueness in Chapter 5.)

Consider a situation in which you believe a worker you're responsible for should either take on additional duties and tasks or hand off some duties or tasks. When you first broach the subject, the worker is hesitant but eventually shows some indication of interest in or willingness to make the change. You become excited about getting what you want. Yet, as a result, the other worker becomes scared, frustrated, or disenchanted and backs up. In that case, what do you do?

- Do you press harder?
- Do you reprimand that worker for going back on his or her first steps?
- Alternatively, do you relax and back off for a moment before inviting that worker to step forward again?

We suggest relaxing or releasing, which allows the other worker to slowly become comfortable with the new situation. In that case, you're allowing that worker to build trust in you, to assume you won't treat him or her poorly or unfairly, but rather, take his or her needs, abilities, and feelings into consideration. Clinton Anderson raises a similar precept in *Clinton Anderson's Lessons Well Learned*: "Do what you have to do to get the job done ... Building better communications with your horse really comes about by making the right things easy and the wrong things difficult – and always rewarding the slightest try."

As you practice "building better communications," how long before you apply more pressure? Wait, at least until after the person has recognized release as a rewarding comfort. As discussed in Chapter 3, people use the "listening" skill of reading unspoken messages in tone of voice and body language. People listen both with their ears and with their eyes. So, if you are listening more with your eyes than your ears, you'll learn when the person has acknowledged the release. Remember, if you are listening, you are in the leadership position and the power position.

Now, consider what release looks like:

- Release is *not* more pressure.
- Release is *not* a sense of false urgency. Even if you are in an emergency situation, showing decisiveness is more effective than showing false urgency.
- Release can include encouraging words or body language. Consider the facial expressions you make when you react to first, desirable steps and feel eager to gain momentum and quick success. Does the urgency you feel, which is typically reflected in your facial expression, send a message

of comfort, security, or appreciation?

- Release can be as simple as a short pause before pushing on to the next step.

What if a person never moves in the desired direction? In solution-focused leadership we follow the principle that there's always a helpful and useful *exceptional moment*. (See Chapter 18 to learn more about exceptional moments.) Sooner or later, in most situations, people will have an exceptional moment and then they will move in the desired direction. This move may not be totally obvious or complete. So, think about this movement on a scale of behavior from one to ten, in which one is the least difficult and ten the most. If you consider the person's former dug-in attitude as a nine, try to recall a time when that attitude was a five or a six. If this exceptional time was in the past, try to remember what you did do or what the circumstances of the exceptional time were. If the exceptional time is in the present, don't overreact by overemphasizing the attitude or behavior related to that time. Instead, try to relax. Let the exceptional moment's attitude sink in. Then, you can apply more pressure to guide the person in the desired direction.

Recall the story at the beginning of Part II. When Talmage would back up Apache, Tim's son was putting pressure on the horse as the consequence for crowding a human. When he sensed Apache was reaching his limit, Talmage would stop backing up the horse. This pause gave Apache a release and helped him understand Talmage's expectations. When Apache exceeded the appropriate space boundaries, Talmage presented consequences to the horse.

HORSE SENSE

*"It's important when working with horses to make
the wrong thing difficult and the right thing easy."*
– Buck Brannaman

In *Believe: A Horseman's Journey*, Buck Brannaman quotes his mentor, Ray Hunt, as saying, "A horse is multitudes of actions and reactions, separate and inseparable, all at the same time." Buck continues:

> It's important when working with horses to make the wrong thing difficult and the right thing easy. That's a philosophy I grew up hearing, and it really works. But be careful not to make the wrong thing completely impossible, because the horse has to have the opportunity to make the mistake in order to learn the lesson. You have to allow horses to search for answers and make their own decisions, and if they make a bad decision, you make corrections ... We also have to be ahead of our horses at all times, to shape things so they can make the right decision without difficulty or fear.

Recall a similar statement in the quotation by Clinton Anderson earlier in this chapter. The importance of this idea appears to be accepted by most horsemen. We suggest you should consider this important idea when dealing with people too. As a supervisor, your job is to use your knowledge of the work, your experience, and your understanding of the principles behind that work to think ahead and prepare your people for what to expect.

CHAPTER 12

IN A NEW WORLD, WE DO
THINGS DIFFERENTLY

---

*When working with a horse, try to use
soft firmness instead of hard tightness.*

W hen working with a horse, try to use a soft
firmness instead of a hard tightness. We take
this principle from revered natural horse trainer
Ray Hunt's *Think Harmony With Horses: An
In-Depth Study of Horse/Man Relationship*. As mentioned in the
preface, we define management as making decisions. We define

supervision as playing a role in making decisions about resources, especially financial and human resources.

Horse trainers use the terms *old-school training* and *natural training*. In discussing management and supervision, we use the terms *Theory X management* and *Theory Y management*, since these approaches to supervision relate to decisions we make and attitudes we have.

In old-school training, cowboys "force," or break, horses by inflicting pain and fear on them. Typically, this manner of training results in the horse obeying and doing what the cowboy wants. As the name suggests, old-school training is how horse training was done in decades past. Many old-school trainers today still rely on tradition or patterns of activities without wavering, like the cowboy illustrated in Chapter 11 working with the horse that just won't move.

By contrast, in natural horse training, the cowboy and the horse forge a relationship that's more of a partnership. According to Jay Brewer, such a partnership isn't quite equal because the horse gets 49 percent of the say and the cowboy gets 51 percent. Still, this partnership is developed and continuously improved upon as the parties learn together about their work and relationship.

Natural horse trainers employ methods of directing horses' behavior based on the animals' natural movements and instincts. A cowboy communicates in ways the horse understands and to which it tends to respond favorably, using both speech (including controlled tone of voice) and body language.

HORSE SENSE

Smart cowboys employ methods of directing behavior based on movements and instincts natural to the horse.

Now, consider how workplace methods have changed over time. In the old days supervisors practiced Theory X management. Theory X, which represents the traditional view of direction and control, relies on the following assumptions:

1. The average person inherently dislikes work and will avoid work if at all possible.
2. Most people need to be coerced, controlled, directed, or threatened with punishment to stimulate adequate work effort.
3. The average person prefers to be directed, wants no responsibility, and has little ambition. Mostly, he or she wants security.

Years ago, Harold received a book of supervision principles by Gen. George Patton. He remembers one of Patton's principles well: "Grab 'em by the nose and kick 'em in the ass." That's Theory X in a nutshell.

Over the last several decades, many supervisors have shifted from "hard" Theory X management approaches to "soft" Theory Y approaches. Theory Y, which represents a more current view of supervision based on participation, consensus, and support, relies on the following assumptions:

1. Most people are good and want to contribute and succeed.
2. Most people can and will improve their performance.
3. The average person will exercise self-direction and self-control to meet expectations he or she buys into.
4. The average person both accepts and seeks responsibility.

In Theory Y, supervisors focus on what works for an individual person. They try to get the best the person has to offer. Theory Y practitioners believe a subordinate wants and can learn to achieve the sought performance. Such a supervisor communicates efforts through speech and body language to encourage people to confidently offer their individual strengths in achieving a shared vision.

Theory X and Theory Y supervision approaches are essentially opposite in nature. If you take one approach, you can't take the other. We still know relatively successful people in high positions who argue they're successful in managing others by creating fear. Through fear of losing their job, being yelled at, or being punished, these people will step up and do what they're told to do. There's no partnership in such a scenario, though. The subordinates may do what they're told, but their supervisor shouldn't expect understanding, creativity, respect, or commitment to the work from them. In other words, the supervisor won't get his or her people's hearts. (We discuss the importance of getting your people to put their hearts into their work in Chapter 6.) Thankfully, the theory and practice of management and supervision are shifting to emphasize establishing security, empowerment, and trust in the workplace.

Consider again the harrowing experience in which Talmage had to regain control over Apache racing through the field. Instinctively, Talmage took a soft, encouraging, and hopeful approach; he did not use a hard, threatening, and fear-oriented approach. He didn't show weakness, fear, or anger. As a result, the soft approach worked, even on a headstrong animal like Apache. Luckily for Talmage, he used this approach intuitively.

Most likely, before coming to Talmage, Apache probably ran away from someone else. Despite his lack of training, Apache had to learn not to run away either from or with his rider. To teach his horse better behavior, Talmage had to use firmness and garner the confidence to take action in the midst of a difficult event.

As mentioned above, many trainers still use the old-school methods on horses. Cowboys brought up on these methods believe they're undertaking training correctly because their approach has worked, to some degree, in the past. (See the discussion of Monty Roberts describing his father as a Theory X-oriented person in Chapter 4.) However, an abundance of evidence demonstrates natural horse training works better than old-school methods do. Today, as younger cowboys are faced with choosing either old-school or natural horse training, most choose natural horse training. Similarly, Theory X sometimes works for supervisors. However, Theory Y has been shown to work much better for a wider spectrum of supervisors, especially in today's world, where subordinates are privy to readily accessible information and want to contribute ideas to their supervisors' decisions.

As shown in this chapter's illustration, and as discussed in the preface, this book is squarely behind the Theory Y supervision approach. We firmly believe in Theory Y's superior results and see a clear correlation between Theory Y and natural horse training. That's why we've chosen to use natural horse training principles to illustrate the Theory Y management, supervision, and leadership principles we discuss. In this illustration, we've relegated those who prefer to use Theory X to the corner of the classroom, since they don't understand the horse's lesson and because they refuse to try to understand Theory Y. Natural horse training and the Theory Y approach to supervision go beyond simply training horses and people to perform duties. Instead, both approaches focus on developing others to their maximum potential.

As we transition from the Theory X to the Theory Y supervision approach, Ray Hunt's principle referenced at the beginning of this chapter – "Instead of a hard tightness, try to find a soft firmness" – fits in well. Ray adds, "It's amazing what the horse can do in spite of the rider." Supervisors aren't being Pollyannaish (that is, illogically optimistic) in their expectation of people's inherent goodness and willingness to try to do their best. Supervisors don't back off from their responsibility to give direction and expect results. They do need to be firm (steadfast, secure, and solid) in supervising other people to be productive members of the team. However, this process is not about hardness, tightness, control, or fear. Instead, it centers on softness, firmness, empowerment, and trust. In *Cowboy Logic*, Ray Hunt reminds readers, "Believe in your horse so your horse can believe in you." You may wonder how this logic would relate to the workplace. Well, if you don't believe in your people, how can they believe in you? How can they believe in themselves?

The current approaches of natural horse training and Theory Y respond to the goodness in horses and in people, respectively. Looking for goodness rather than expecting badness is a more joyful way to go about life. Manage and supervise for the best in people rather than the worst. We believe everything you do to help producers to produce will help shirkers to shirk, while everything you do to keep shirkers from shirking will keep producers from producing. (We discuss producers and shirkers in more detail in Chapter 19.) You get to choose which approach to take. For us, we choose to help producers and look for the goodness in people, all while realizing a firm hand must be applied. We want to help producers produce while encouraging shirkers not to shirk.

CHAPTER 13
IT'S ABOUT CHANGE

Prepare your horse to respond favorably
in any set of circumstances.

P repare your horse to respond favorably in any set of circumstances. Did you ever want someone who works for you to change or to be a different person? Wouldn't it be helpful if the same people would have the right perspective, ideas, focus, skills, behaviors, and relationships with clients and coworkers? In this context, "right" is what makes sense to each of us, of course.

We live in a world of frequent and regular change. Whatever you plan to do today may change tomorrow. Whatever you expected for your life will, most likely, change. Even so, precious few of us embrace or eagerly anticipate change. Most folks would prefer some consistency and constancy. Yet, undoubtedly, change is what everyone gets. Supervisors and leaders need to understand the complexities of change and do what they can to position their people and organizations for change.

You can start the process of dealing with change by positioning yourself and your team for the transition. In *Cowboy Logic*, Ray Hunt is crisp on this point: "You prepare for the transition." People tend to be uncomfortable with and even frightened by uncertainty, and change indicates uncertainty. Thus, a supervisor's job is to bring as much certainty as possible to the changes he or she asks the team to make.

You might think what people need to do is teach others to "suck it up" and deal with change, since change is a fact of life. Yet most people want to know what to do and how to deal with change. As you help those you work with deal with change, where should you start?

While change often catches folks unprepared, leaders, supervisors, and managers must anticipate change. Moreover, they must learn what their people need in order to be prepared. Supervisors can prepare and position their people for change by being explicit about the anticipated change's purpose, potential gains, potential losses, and potential opportunities.

While supervisors usually ask for change for very good reasons, most people find change difficult because their routines and comfort levels are being challenged. The precise reason for any change, whether it's improving the workplace or the work process, or closing gaps in culture, funding, or technical capability, isn't the issue. People must constantly adapt to changes in the business environment, especially since business environment changes beget other changes. Just because a change is valuable doesn't mean everyone on the team agrees with or wants it. However, people will be much more receptive if they're ready and positioned to accept the reasoning for and the methods needed to achieve the change. As supervisor, your job is to understand the change you're asking your staff to make, determine how best to position your staff for that change, and build consensus on how best to achieve that change. Think of this in relative terms: people don't dislike change as much as they dislike another person trying to change them.

Consider five aspects of positioning for change.

- First is *definition*. You need to clearly define what the change is and its purpose – why you're asking for change – so your people understand what you're asking. (As we discuss in Chapter 16, people find comfort in clarity.)
- Second is *direction*. You need to clearly communicate what the change will bring. What will the work or the workplace be like after the change is complete? Purpose and direction define your goal.
- Third is *place*. Consider where you start the change. Determine what the first step is in taking the team from the place where you start the change toward the desired goal.
- Fourth is *acquiring resources*. Determine what you need to support making the change and what you need to accommodate the change.

- Fifth is *method*.[4] Consider how the team can use the available resources to yield the change you want.

As you direct a team's positioning change, you may set a wonderful goal and have good intent, but that's not enough. In addition, you must provide the appropriate resources and methods for the people who will achieve the goal.

To direct someone toward change, you must define and communicate your vision (that is, the result to which the desired change leads). To support a person's effort to change, you need to go to where that other person is. You can't support people's efforts to achieve a vision if you don't understand what they see when they look toward that vision. So, of course, as a supervisor, you have to be a good listener. You need to learn how each team member understands the vision and his or her role in achieving that vision. Each person has dreams, talents, strengths, resources, and a unique worldview. A good supervisor needs to ensure everyone on the team has a common understanding of the vision and the means by which that vision can and will become reality.

As supervisor, you want each team member's understanding of the change to be made and the need for change to be in concert with your vision. In addition, you want each person to move toward your vision for the work and the workplace. You need to support the team members in finding and using their unique strengths and abilities as they move toward the vision.

When you ask for change, you're expecting people to carry out tactical and operational activities based on your strategy and vision.

---

[4]Total quality management guru W. Edwards Deming, who's generally credited for transforming Japan after World War II, would always ask the question, "By what method?" (We mention Deming's profound question in Chapter 6.)

- Setting goals, directions, and purposes are strategic activities.
- Determining and providing resources are tactical activities.
- Providing and implementing processes or procedures for using the resources in achieving the goals are operational activities.

Within a team, the people who are responsible for strategic activities are apt to embrace change, since vision and strategy are future-oriented (as are the results of change). In turn, the people responsible for tactical and operational activities are more apt to put up with and perhaps even challenge change because they're unsure about the availability of needed resources and methods. When people don't have the resources and the methods to do what's expected of them, they are more reluctant to change. A supervisor's job is to provide the resources and the methods, along with the ability (that is, giving the training) to understand and use the resources and methods.

Returning to the idea of natural horse training, when asking his horse to change direction, a cowboy is concerned about making sure the horse's feet and body are positioned correctly. He wants the horse's eyes and thoughts focused on the goal, which is the new direction. He wants the horse's attitude to be positive and eager. In short, to accommodate change, horses need solid foundations and stability in order to start toward uncertainty and imbalance. For example, in the story at the beginning of Part II, Tim and Talmage had to work hard to provide Apache with foundation and stability, since a previous owner had left the horse uncertain and imbalanced. The family created this foundation and stability by setting boundaries and expectations for Apache. Similarly, people need to be sure of a solid foundation and stability when embarking on uncertainty and imbalance created by change.

Jay Brewer's contemplation of the speaking element of communication is something useful for all of us to think about. He considers whether he's *asking* something of the horse or *telling* the horse to do something. On Jay's part, the difference between the two is similar to the difference between kissing and slapping. Kissing is asking. Slapping is telling. When Jay asks a horse to pay attention or move a certain way, he makes a kissing sound. When the horse doesn't respond appropriately, Jay slaps the horse's neck. Of course, the horse can barely feel Jay's slap, but the horse can see and hear the more commanding sound. Clearly, when using the kissing and slapping method, a cowboy is communicating with his horse: the cowboy is listening to the horse and the horse is listening to the cowboy.

Used together by a cowboy training his horse, kissing and slapping can work effectively. Jay says, "Ask, ask, ask, then tell, then create an uncomfortable situation. Intensify the asking, then tell, and when necessary tell so they [the horses] become uncomfortable." One rule we've learned for good management (from our experiences with horses, in business, and in the military) is that you have to tell someone something three times for the idea to take. Perhaps the three-times rule applies to asking as well. Was it coincidence that Jay said, "Ask, ask, ask?"

HORSE SENSE

You have to tell someone something three times for it to take.

The point is to ask several times. At that juncture, if you don't get the response to the change you need, then take the directing stance. Following that, if there is still no response, you can make the situation around the unwanted or unhelpful behavior uncomfortable. This last idea is popular with many natural horse trainers. Buck Brannaman discusses many examples in which he has used this technique successfully, such as in the following instance:

> I'll ... pick a goal for my herd-bound horse, a spot under a shady tree at the end of the meadow or some distant corner ... I simply cause movement. What I'm doing is making what he [the horse] thought was a good place to be – the herd – a little difficult for him. I want him to understand that being alone with me in the corner of the pasture or under the shady tree is where he'll find the most security and comfort.

People aren't that different from horses in this respect. Supervisors need to find ways to encourage team members who want to do their best and to recognize ways to bring these people security and comfort.

The horse-training notion of kissing (as asking) and slapping (as telling) might also be an important concept for leading people. In recognizing another person's strengths, a good supervisor should ask more than he or she tells. As mentioned in Chapter 1, many people have trouble listing their strengths. In fact, people often find they have previously undiscovered strengths, and they can and will bring those strengths to the table when a leader recognizes and affirms those strengths. When supervisors ask, they lift a person up and show their respect for him or her. When supervisors tell, they diminish the person and show their position of authority. Often, but not always, this is a useful influence.

Be certain to distinguish between when you ask and when you tell. People tend to tell most of the time, when they should be asking more. You don't learn much through telling. Rather, you can learn much more through asking. Part of effective listening is asking open questions, which help make space for those answering to go to wherever they need to go, and asking circular questions, which help those answering to be more thorough when they discuss the issue. Circular and open questions invite more information about the topic you, the questioner, have just reflected upon. Open questions make space and circular questions follow up. In each case, be certain you made sure you have understood by using effective reflection (recall Chapter 3).

However, those for whom you're responsible need to know when you want their input – that is, their participative decision making and new ideas – or when you want their output – that is, their dedicated effort leading to results. (The latter is humorously expressed in a dog-related analogy: "head down, butt up, scratch dirt.") Asking leads to input, while telling leads to output. Good supervisors must ensure their people know whether they are asking for input or telling output.

There's more to positioning for a transition than the physical positioning described above. Horses and people also respond to emotional positioning. Both horses and people react emotionally to change through their mammalian brain (the limbic system). (We discuss the limbic system in more detail in Chapter 22.) When supervisors ask for change, they tend to drive the change through mental and organizational forces, such as new policies, corporate action, and extrinsic motivation (that is, the carrot and the stick). In response, those being asked to change resist because of personal and emotional restraining forces, such as confusion, anxiety, and dislike of perceived coercion. The more supervisors push on the driving forces, the more they receive the restraining forces. *The key to change is dealing with the personal or emotional restraining forces.*

When supervisors ask for change, they must deal with what team members perceive to be the loss of the "normal" and the fear of failure they may be experiencing. While people may not dislike change, they dislike others trying to change them. Instead of only trying to rally people around the beneficial results of change, a good supervisor can address the loss of the familiar – that is, the current or known reality – and the emotions involved as the team prepares for change. Sometimes, the perceived losses may seem inconsequential:

- People may fear losing part of their work ritual.
- They may fear losing relationships with other people in the workplace.
- They may fear losing an office's geographic proximity to conveniences such as the lunchroom, the bathroom, or the elevators.
- They may lose hope of contributing suggestions and ideas and, by extension, influencing the change.

At a minimum, good supervisors can help team members work through these seemingly inconsequential but often emotionally powerful losses by encouraging discussions that are characterized by the important skill of reflection, reconnect people with the vision, and help them move on.

When a change makes good sense, it's easier to convince oneself to change. Supervisors need to share their thinking and take time to explain why each change is important – that is, not just the what, but the so-what – how and when the transition will be accomplished, and what the anticipated results of making the change will be. In other words, this aids people who are, for the most part, uncomfortable with perceived *reactionary* change and are more comfortable with perceived *planned* change.

Kurt Lewin, a recognized pioneer in the development of change management, said to effectively manage change, people have to deal with ending the old (*unfreezing*), transitioning to the new, and accepting the new (*refreezing*). The primary reason for failure in organizational change is ignoring the endings. People grieve the loss of perceived advantages of their old ways.

Unfreezing, or ending the old, is the key foundational step for anyone asking for a transition. In short, supervisors and team members have to position their minds, emotions, and bodies so everyone is prepared when the transition occurs. Similarly, a horse needs a solid foundation and stability in order to move toward uncertainty and imbalance.

When Apache wanted to run back to the barn, Talmage had to bring about change and learn how to unfreeze his horse. Then, Talmage used the right amount of pressure and transitioned Apache into behaving under control. Over time, Talmage managed to teach Apache new, desirable behavior and refreeze the horse there.

For Apache, and for the rest of us, the unfreezing is the hardest part. So, as we move on to the next chapter, consider the following question: in what ways might you unfreeze your people and organization to position everyone for change?

CHAPTER 14

KNOW THE PROCESS

---

*Your horse needs to be aware of each
and every step of the process.*

Your horse needs to be aware of each and every step of
the process. At each step, he needs to know his role, his
responsibility, and what to expect from the cowboy. In
addition, the horse needs to know *every part* of the total
job, how those parts work together, and what the expected outcome
is. Of course, the horse's knowledge of every part isn't equivalent to

what a person's knowledge for completing a job might be. However, the horse still needs to be given an appropriate pace and sense of accomplishment as he works through the steps of the process in completing the parts of the total job.

When considering the above principle and applying it to the workplace, keep three thoughts in mind:

1. Be aware of each and every step of the process you use to do your job.
2. Strive to make what you're doing as efficient and effective as possible.
3. Communicate what you know.

We can effectively discuss the parts of what people do on the job by defining what makes good workflow and management processes. A good workflow process has steps in the right sequence. It also includes the tools and skills needed to perform those steps. A good management process enables supervisors to gather information and make decisions about how to do the steps of the workflow process well. Together, the workflow and management processes help people gain control of life and work. Stated simply, people need to know the appropriate methods to get the envisioned results.

In *Think Harmony with Horses*, Ray Hunt says he believes the cowboy is the leader in a dance in which the horse and rider should move with rhythm and harmony. In any successful dance, both partners need to know their steps and how the steps progress from one to the next. When people have practiced the dance enough, they know what to expect next and how to relate to their partners at specific times within the dance sequence. Without a mutually understood process, dancers can step on each other's toes. Individuals need to be aware of each and every step and movement to complete the dance or the job successfully.

Natural horse trainer Louis Wood expands on the importance of good timing: "It's not how long you've worked with the horse, it's doing the right thing at the right time." To know how to do the right thing at the right time, supervisors and team members need to know, intimately, the sequence of steps leading to the objective. As individuals perform a task a number of times, they internalize the process by which they've accomplished the task.

HORSE SENSE

"It's not how long you've worked with the horse, it's doing the right thing at the right time."
– Louis Wood

The idea of process is important in the workplace, not just on horseback. A process "conduces to an end." That is, when people understand a process, they know the beginning, the end, and the steps in between. A process "conduces" when people faithfully follow the steps, as defined in the process, and achieve that process's predictable end. So, when people define a process, they need to make sure they've identified a desired end.

Some professionals, most notably, systems engineers, center their thinking on process. Systems engineers believe if people develop the right process and faithfully follow that process, they'll achieve the desired end. However, the right process isn't always obvious. Therefore, people usually have to keep an open mind about any process and continually improve it in order to achieve more efficient results. Because a process exists in an environment of changing constraints and new opportunities, it will need to be changed to adjust to new constraints and to improve efficiency within old constraints.

When defining a new process or improving an existing process, start by looking at a relevant, currently used process. Whether by design or by default, people follow a process with steps for any task they do. Over time, most people settle on a process they follow consistently, based on habit. Once a process becomes a habit, people tend to follow that process, regardless of its practicality or appropriateness, instead of choosing a new or different, less familiar process. You may have noticed that your staff will also tend to settle on their own habitual processes. As manager, supervisor, or leader, you need to understand the entire process, even though that may not be easy. The people who do the work and perform the steps (seldom the supervisor) know best what those steps are.

When you're trying to identify the steps in your current process, an interesting situation arises. If two people who do a similar process are asked to describe it, each person will typically report different steps. The two may even argue over the proper steps or order. You'll want to walk through and personally observe the process as the steps are being performed. At this point, the best approach is to document the steps of the process. Technical people tend to prefer diagrams showing the process, while nontechnical people tend to prefer written steps detailing a procedure. Either way, make sure you capture actions, decisions, or branching-off points, along with points where you need to input or access information.

Once you've clearly defined the current process, you can identify inefficiencies, wasted efforts and steps, gaps and overlaps, ineffective communication, and conflicting or redundant information. When you have a list of these difficulties, you're armed to improve the process. At that point, you should document the improved process, taking into account the corrections you've chosen with the intent of resolving the difficulties. Then, you can address those difficulties as process improvement steps, which can be taken later as time and resources allow. This step-focused approach to process improvement is less intimidating because the focus is on the steps – that is, on the process – and not the person undergoing those steps.

Both people and horses tend to be comfortable with the currently implemented or "old" ways of doing things, whether those ways are best or not. A cowboy must be eternally vigilant in identifying unhelpful behaviors in a horse; he must repeatedly lead the horse through more helpful behaviors. In contrast, a supervisor should encourage team members to achieve more helpful behaviors and solutions on their own. Since humans have the unique capacity for imagining what doesn't exist, you and your work team should be able to find ways to help people visualize what an improved process means for them. At that point, you must address emotional responses to any change, as discussed in Chapter 13.

The good news for people is they have the capacity to visualize every part of a job and should be able to see how each part relates to the overall process. Then, they can understand how expending extra effort to improve one part of the process can make life much better when undertaking subsequent parts. The key here is to provide folks with good visualization tools and clear process definitions. If you give people the time they need to understand the differences between the current process steps and the new steps, which have been designed to yield improvement in work and results, you'll find your staff accepting and implementing those needed changes.

For both people in the workplace and for cowboys and their horses, repeating a process leads to internalization and comprehension of expectations. Once people or horses determine an effective process, they want to work on the process, which will lead each team to desired results.

Think back to the story of Talmage and Apache. As Talmage improved his riding skills and more fully understood the processes needed to ride well and safely, Apache's bad habits decreased. Over time, the rider-horse team's ability to complete work tasks successfully increased. A well-defined and well-implemented process gave Apache competence, confidence, and comfort to correctly do his job. Generally, the exciting outcome of developing and following an effective process is reaping the benefits of knowing what to do beforehand and recognizing how what you have done in the process has led to success. In Talmage and Apache's case, the two found success in a partnership when they reached their relationship's full potential.

As a final example of the ideas discussed in this chapter, let's turn to the experiences of Harold's wife, Pamela, a creative, decisive, and caring university administrator. You'd think she would rather not follow the defined steps of any process. However, over time, she came to love the process she used for management, supervision, and leadership in her work. When using her process, she found great joy in its inherent benefits. She loved the process for the freedom it gave her, a hugely creative person, to be creative. In addition, using the process gave Pamela's bosses confidence in her management abilities, since she could always give them accurate numbers and tell them where she stood in her work. Since, by using the process, Pamela could always justify resources and rewards for supervisees' work and results, her direct reports had confidence in her leadership. Because she had a firm grasp on the present and knew the lessons of the past,

Pamela could lead discussions about the future. Her process gave her control of her life and work.

CHAPTER 15

WHAT HAPPENED?

*Get your horse to look at what led
to something happening.*

G et your horse to look at what led to something happening. We believe all events or results telegraph themselves. Any event starts out small. That small beginning is "what happened *before*." Before what? Before whatever it was that happened *happened* – that is, whatever took place before the major event or end result. Most people tend to ignore the small things, or dismiss them as unimportant. However, the small things often evolve into larger things. If people continue to ignore these things or dismiss their significance, what starts as a small thing may become a big disaster.

Harold's favorite example of small things telegraphing themselves and, if left unattended, becoming disasters involves the time one summer when he was burning brush. As Harold cleared more and more land to landscape the grounds of his family's country inn, the brush pile, placed at the edge of a no-till cornfield, had grown. In no-till planting, instead of plowing a field, people plant ryegrass in the fall, chemically kill the ryegrass in the spring, and then, in an effort to prevent erosion, cut small slits a couple of inches deep into the loose dirt and drop the seeds (in this case, corn kernels) at the tip of each cut. One day, Harold set the family's brush pile on fire and took refuge in the shade at the edge of the woods bordering the cornfield. He wanted to watch and make sure the fire didn't spread toward the woods.

After a while, Harold discovered a spark had gotten into the dead ryegrass some distance from the woods. This small event telegraphed a larger, potential problem that would have been very easy to resolve: Harold could have simply stomped out the spark. Yet, because Harold didn't catch the spark in time, it had become a flame in the grass. At this point, the flame would have been a bit more difficult to extinguish, but it could have been put out with some stomping around. Unfortunately, because he was at the edge of the woods, Harold missed both the spark and the initial flame.

So, what Harold really discovered was a ring of fairly low flame, measuring about 15 feet in diameter, on the burning brush pile's field side. To make a long story short, Harold couldn't stomp fast enough or long enough to put out the fire. He had to race to call the fire department and get experts to put out the fire before the flames reached the woods on the distant, far side of the field.

Thus, a simple spark, which started rather mildly, became a fire because it went unnoticed and unattended. Because he didn't deal with the flames early enough, Harold ended up with a disaster. Fixing that disaster required resources to which he didn't readily have access. This type of situation occurs in the workplace all the time. So, supervisors have to be aware of the possibility of and the potential for difficulties. They have to look at what *could* happen before it happens, and they definitely have to do so before the event gets out of hand. In *Cowboy Logic*, Ray Hunt describes this principle with a question: "What happened before what you want to have happen happened?"

Yet how do you look at what happened *before* an event took place? You need to use your imagination and start anticipating what could happen before events take their course. You can use other people's experiences, but that is often very difficult. Alternatively, you can imagine what might not go exactly the way you expect. However, it's pretty hard to anticipate difficulties in a new process. So, what strategies can you use to overcome such a hurdle? Take small steps, monitor everything very closely, and check actual results against anticipated results on a regular and frequent basis. In other words, watch carefully and be prepared to act when the spark, whatever it is, appears.

Truly understanding and learning how to manage processes and people around this principle can make a huge difference in the workplace, since not catching a problem in its infancy can turn it into an even bigger problem. Suppose you didn't measure or monitor the basic metrics of your work, and you missed a spark. The spark became a flame and then a brush fire. Since you didn't have ready resources to deal with the disaster, you had to call on your colleagues to pitch in and help you douse the flames. At that point, your colleagues became distracted from their own work and missed sparks of their own. Their sparks became flames and then forest fires, and they had to call for help. This condition is called "discontinuity of organization." Due to a lack of focused attention, the organization breaks down into continuous brush fires.

Imagine if Talmage hadn't addressed Apache's crowding issue because the rider wasn't really bothered by the horse's close proximity or just thought it was sweet. This little spark could have become a forest fire, figuratively speaking, had Apache knocked Talmage over and stepped on him.

A memorable way to state the condition of not recognizing what happened before an event blew up is the notion of "nits, gnats, and tanks." Problems don't start off big. They start off small, say, about the size of a nit (a louse egg, which is very, *very* small). People don't always know what to look for. Often, they try to ignore a small problem, hoping it will go away. Yet, as Harold learned from his brush fire experience, undetected or unaddressed details can have a big impact. Any problem first appears as a nit. Yet, since people tend to ignore or put off dealing with such small problems, the next thing they know, that nit-sized issue has become a pesky, more threatening gnat. If no one deals effectively with the problem, the team is likely to face a tank, or a very big problem, coming through the office door.

Admiral Hyman Rickover, father of the nuclear navy, coined the phrase, "The devil is in the details, but so is the salvation." Supervision involves paying attention to details. Good supervision involves paying attention to the right details. Bad supervision, sometimes called micromanagement, involves paying attention to the wrong details. So, who knows what the right details are? Those who do the work and are closest to the details usually know the right ones to focus on. What's more, they will tell you, their leader, what the right detail is – if they trust you.

In that situation, the leader may know where we want to be (WWWTB) and therefore where the team members need to go. However, those closer to the work are more likely to know how to get there (HTGT) – that is, what to do. (We explain these acronyms in Chapters 16 and 20.) Other team members are more familiar with the situation "on the ground" and what the opportunities and difficulties in meeting the vision may be. Since these others will provide the needed information to the leader if there is trust, a good leader should create a work environment in which there is trust (see Chapters 17 and 22 for a more in-depth discussion on trust).

People need attitudes, guides, tools, and processes to help them pay attention to the right details. Good supervisors need the right details about the right things at the right time and in the right place. To get those details, they need to understand the process, and they can gain deeper understanding of the process from their staff members.

In supervising and managing their responsibilities, supervisors need to keep on top of the details, even those they find tedious or boring. Effective supervisors don't let nits become gnats, and they definitely don't let nits or gnats grow into tanks. For example, as a project manager, if you're not paying attention to the financial details of your work every week, you'll miss the nits and maybe even the gnats. Later on, because of the tank you've gotten, you may believe you need to focus on dealing with it (that is, with your crisis) and don't have time to spend looking for new nits. At that point, it's quite likely you're dealing with discontinuity of organization.

In the workplace, each brush fire comes from one small spark. If people don't look for the spark or are distracted from the spark, flames soon appear. If the small flames don't lead to wild grass fires, people have luck to thank. (In Harold's case, it's really lucky the grass fire didn't burn down the country inn.) So, pay attention to those nits. For learning purposes, think back to these ideas the next time you encounter a workplace crisis. Figure out when the problem first appeared, as a nit, and recall why you chose not to deal with it or didn't recognize it for what it was.

In a broader sense, true leaders look forward, not backward, in the workplace. They have experience to lean on as they use their ability to look into the future. They're not caught up in figuring out what's going on right in the moment. Instead, true leaders are aware of history and what has happened to get them to a particular point. They respect the past and those who have knowledge of that past. Yet, just as a saddle only faces one way, leaders don't dwell on what happened in the past. Instead, they look for possibility. Leaders consider future opportunities and consequences. Then, they determine what they need to decide or do in the moment to help themselves later take advantage of those opportunities or mitigate unfavorable consequences. Overall, leaders must be vigilant, remaining ever mindful of potential small problems and of future opportunities. Both problems and opportunities are challenges, and leaders are great at dealing with challenges.

If you listen carefully in the workplace, you'll hear about or notice signs pointing to a potential problem before that problem happens. The people closest to the action in the workplace know what's going on and what the difficulties are. If trust has been established (a topic we discuss at length in Chapters 17 and 22), these people will communicate their information to the leader. The issue of providing the leader with the information he or she needs to guide the direction and support the effort to get to the vision is described

by Louis Wood in horse-and-cowboy terms: "The horse will 'say' that [something's] not going to work – you've got to pay attention to your horse." As always, communication depends on effective listening on the leader's (or cowboy's) part and requires the leader to pay close attention to those for whom he or she is responsible.

The natural horse trainer generally recognized as the person who most affected the development of the effective listening approach is the late Tom Dorrance. Along with his brother, Bill, Tom Dorrance inspired a genealogy of natural horsemanship trainers that reaches from Ray Hunt and Buck Brannaman to most modern horse trainers. In *True Unity: Willing Communication Between Horse and Human*, Tom writes:

> Some riders I have worked with are getting closer and closer to feeling the feet, and where they are, and what is going to happen before it even happens. If the horse [needs] a little support, a little directing, a little help, they are more ready to help the horse at the time the horse needs it. If the horse is going to make it anyway, these riders don't get in the way, and that is so important.

In other words, learning comes from trying to do things at the edge of one's ability. Leaders give their people space to try. Even if there's a problem, as long as a rider knows the horse will get though it without harm – even if the horse has to struggle – the rider should let the horse get through the problem on its own. Similarly, a leader has to know what's going to teach his or her staff more: not facing a problem or working through managed problems. *Managed problems* may mean personal sacrifice on the part of the staff that shouldn't affect critical budget or schedule items. In these cases, it may be best to just let events happen, even if you can avoid them and have predicted them, while remaining ready, willing, and able to step in, if necessary, to avoid disaster.

HORSE SENSE

If there's a problem, as long as a rider knows the horse will get though it without harm — even if the horse has to struggle — the rider should let the horse get through the problem on its own.

Let's return to Dorrance's statement about the cowboy and his or her horse, which applies to a supervisor and his or her direct report. As that supervisor, if you're aware of and care about those you work with, you'll be able to interpret where they are and what may be about to happen with them before any events occur. A supervisor should be responsive with the right mix of support, direction, and help. When it's best to get out of the way of a person who's headed in the right direction, supervisors shouldn't overdo it. A true leader stays out of the way when his or her direct report is headed slightly off-course. That's because the leader knows the direct report will learn a meaningful lesson and will self-correct if allowed to continue in his or her own direction. Sometimes, hidden strengths can be discovered along the way.

In the case of the cowboy and the horse, the horse knows what the details for implementing the vision are. When the cowboy can listen with senses more acute than physical hearing, he will "hear" what his horse is "saying." For instance, Talmage learned to listen to Apache and determine whether the horse was exhibiting bad behaviors or successfully using new, learned, good behaviors. Because Talmage and Apache were able to develop a good relationship based on mutual trust, Talmage was able to consider events before they happened because he understood how his horse would react to many given circumstances.

CHAPTER 16
WE PERFORM BEST WITH COMFORT AND CLARITY

Encourage your horse to be comfortable with what's expected while you remain confident about its ability to be successful.

E
ncourage your horse to be comfortable with what's expected while you remain confident about its ability to be successful. By and large, horses and people will steer away from anything that causes them to feel uncomfortable and steer toward anything that causes them to feel comfortable.

Most individuals, whether horses or people, find situations are easier to face when they have confidence in their ability to overcome potential obstacles. Therefore, a sense of competence offers comfort to the horse and to the person. So, how do good leaders encourage others to develop feelings of competence, confidence, optimism, perceived control, purpose, trust, self-esteem, accountability, and causality? Supervisors or leaders have a significant, direct effect on the environment their staff experiences. Leaders' behavior sets the tone for the whole place. Through the use of careful, focused thought and diligent action, leaders can create a favorable, encouraging, and joyful environment that encourages their staff to be creative and optimistic in their pursuits, thereby willing to develop their skills and strengths to their maximum potential.

Over the years, we've observed the following behaviors in leaders and supervisors who've successfully created this type of environment.

1. Live with integrity and honor.
2. Be authentic and genuine in your expression of feelings.
3. Exhibit optimism and reduce helplessness on the job.
4. Move from entitlement thinking into entrepreneurial thinking and an abundance mentality (in which you accept opportunities for win-win solutions).
5. Deal with accountability and authority from within yourself.
6. Set an exemplary example; be a great role model.
7. Build competency in your people through training and opportunity.
8. Ask for help, input, and advice in solving problems.
9. Provide space for your people to grow while giving them the freedom and resources to do so.
10. Actively demonstrate your focus on achieving a lofty vision.

11. Develop a closed set (each item is necessary and all items taken together are sufficient).
12. Set short-term expectations for achievable tasks.
13. Coach diligently; use reflection and encouragement skills.
14. Understand the power of encouragement.
15. Review tangible evidence of accomplishments.
16. Give immediate, favorable feedback.
17. Be willing to accept some failures.
18. Be open and honest with information.
19. Communicate supportively. Remember the following communication techniques:
    a. Stay face-to face.
    b. Use active receiving (listening and reading).
    c. Use active sending (speaking and writing).
    d. Pay close attention to nonverbal cues (93 percent of each message sent is conveyed through tone of voice, facial expression, and body language).
    e. Engage in crisp, noiseless communication.
20. Develop interdependent relationships.

Some of these behaviors have been or will be topics for entire chapters in this book, such as understanding the power of encouragement (Chapter 8) and communicating supportively (Chapter 3). You may benefit from further explanation regarding other behaviors, including the following (repeated from the above list):

- Live with integrity and honor.
- Be authentic and genuine in your expression of feelings.
- Move from entitlement thinking into entrepreneurial thinking and an abundance mentality.

- Set an exemplary example; be a great role model.
- Build competency in your people through training and opportunity.
- Set short-term expectations for achievable tasks.
- Be willing to accept some failures.
- Develop interdependent relationships.

So, let's take these behaviors and address them one by one.

First, **living with integrity and honor** means more than abiding by clichés such as "walking the walk" and "telling the truth." Integrity means:

1. You know what you think and feel, based on personal introspection and assessment.
2. You clearly and appropriately communicate your thoughts and feelings.
3. You appropriately follow through with behaviors to implement your thoughts and feelings.

If you live with integrity and honor, you're honest and comfortable with yourself and with others. Honor means you never lie, cheat, or steal, even a little or in small ways. You don't lie to protect yourself, cheat at card games, exaggerate expenses on your income tax, or steal someone's precious time through unhelpful activities, such as wasteful meetings.

Second, if you try to **be authentic and genuine in your expression of feelings**, then you know who you are and what you stand for. To make sure, ask yourself: "Who am I, really?" Determine whether you know what you stand for and believe in, and how you conduct yourself when the chips are down. If you are authentic, you're consistently and firmly yourself. People may not agree with all you want, with your ideas, or with the best way to reach your vision or implement your ideas. Still, they know what your vision, ideas, and methods are; they also know that what they see (or hear) with you is what they get. In knowing these things, other people recognize you as authentic. Your authenticity leads people into clear understanding and comfort, since they know what to expect.

Third, challenge yourself to **move from entitlement thinking into entrepreneurial thinking and an abundance mentality**. The idea of abundance mentality comes from Stephen Covey's *The Seven Habits of Highly Effective People*, in which he considers each situation a win-win opportunity. A win-lose situation may be exciting for some people, but such a situation is uncomfortable for everyone else. When you see win-win in almost every situation, you have developed an abundance mentality. When you focus on the favorable in each situation, you make that situation more comfortable for all parties.

Fourth, remember that **setting an exemplary example and building competency in your people** go together and can be implemented as training through role modeling. Training through role modeling combines instruction with demonstration. During instruction, explain to people – as cowboys demonstrate to horses – what the steps for accomplishing a task are (the what) and why they're important (the so-what). In demonstration, walk those who look to you for cues through the steps of what you're asking them to learn and do. For supervisors, demonstration means they need to perform the activity they are asking of other workers along with those workers, step by step.

Fifth, be mindful that holding **short-term expectations for achievable tasks** means setting proximal expectations for readily achievable tasks. This way, a supervisor can help team members increase their competency one achievable level of accomplishment at a time. This type of behavior is especially powerful. We believe a supervisor can work with the most reluctant (or least confident, or maybe even lazy) person and elevate that person's confidence, participation, and, eventually, contribution to the vision or organization. To do so, a supervisor dedicates time, attention, and process steps to the reluctant person. Step-by-step, the person improves. However, as a supervisor, you may not have time and energy to devote to a single, reluctant person, given the others for whom you're responsible and the activities your team needs to accomplish. As a supervisor, you have to decide how much time and effort you can afford to spend on each reluctant person.

In Talmage and Apache's story, Tim had to decide how much time and energy to put into retraining Apache, given the unexpected challenges and potential benefits for Talmage posed by working with the horse. Tim spent time and energy to ensure Talmage was safe and was also learning from Apache, given the horse's limitations. When Talmage outgrew his horse, Tim had the wisdom to let Apache go to a place where the animal's strengths would fit a new need. Then, he found a new horse for Talmage.

This type of dilemma happens in the workplace more than most people would like. As an organization grows, some people can't keep up with that organization's needs. Such a situation can be disheartening and extremely sad. Sometimes, the very people who were instrumental in helping establish that organization are bypassed as the organization grows in size and expands its capabilities beyond the original team members' strengths. In such cases, the kind thing to do is discover an environment for those people in which they can feel good about their contributions.

Returning to the above list of essential behaviors for successful leaders, you must **be willing to accept some failures.** This idea may be difficult to understand. The type of failure described here is not one of failing to meet a commitment or an expectation; instead, it is a failure at the edge of your understanding, where, naturally, failure readily occurs. Even when people are at the edge of their abilities and try to do their best, they won't always do well. From such failures, people learn and grow. In those professions where failing is disastrous (heart surgery comes to mind), we want people to be working well within their ability. At one point, Harold was responsible for a 235-person research and development organization. Ironically, in that context, if someone he was leading or supervising *never* failed, Harold didn't have a place for that person. Research and development is centered on discovery, which occurs at the edge of our understanding, the very place where we can experience failure.

This idea is true in horsemanship too. Clinton Anderson supports the acceptance of making mistakes, saying, "Correcting a mistake after it occurs accelerates a horse's learning, while preventing a mistake just guarantees he will keep making it."

Finally, as a good leader, you must remember to **develop interdependent relationships**. *Inter*dependence is neither dependence nor independence. Instead, with interdependence, people depend on each other and share power as a team. The most effective way to develop strong feelings of interdependence is through communication. In turn, the most important part of communication is effective listening (discussed in more depth in Chapter 3), and the key to effective listening is reflecting the message the speaker sends to the speaker's satisfaction.

The above behaviors demonstrate a leader's intentions to provide comfort and clarity in the workplace. The importance of clarity can't be stated strongly enough. Supervisors need to communicate directly, specifically, and crisply. When leaders' needs are "gray" (that is, neither black nor white), people are confused, frustrated, and lose their trust in those leaders. Since people will live up to what's expected of them, leaders should be clear in what they expect. One definition of success is simply meeting expectations. To meet expectations, first people must know, with certainty, what those expectations are. Clarity may be the biggest contributor to people's peace and comfort, just as it is to horses.

Some riders might think they need to reward horses with tangible treats. A responsible cowboy realizes treats are nice, but there's more he can offer. More than anything, he can offer a horse clarity about what's expected, how to get there, and how to determine progress. In the words of Louis Wood, "Don't give the horse treats out of hand. The biggest treat is no gray area, NO nonclarity."

Use the acronyms decoded in the box to help your people stay on track. (We mentioned two of these acronyms in Chapter 15, but we define them more carefully here.)

ACRONYM DECODER

- **WWWTB**: Where We Want to Be
- **WWA**: Who We Are; Where We Are
- **HTGT**: How to Get There
- **HTEP**: How to Evaluate Progress

Let's look more closely at these, one at a time:

WWWTB: Where we want to be. This idea is best expressed as a vision, a goal, an objective, or a milestone.

WWA (1): Who we are. Determine whether the team members know their strengths and expectations.

WWA (2): Where we are. How to get from where we are (WWA) to where we want to be (WWWTB) is sometimes designated as HTGT.

HTGT: How to get there. This idea is expressed through mission, strategy, roles and responsibilities, or process steps.

HTEP: How to evaluate progress. HTEP is expressed through success indicators, outcome measures, output measures, or task results.

Supervisors and leaders not only determine the concepts described in these acronyms; they also must effectively communicate them to the people with whom they work. These people make the expectations come true through the appropriate processes, yielding consequences that can lead to a determination of success or failure. Thus, clarity is vitally important.

HORSE SENSE

Let your idea become the horse's idea.

People and horses want comfortable and peaceful environments in which they can focus on what they want to do. The key is for your subordinates (or for a cowboy's horses) to want to do what you want them to do. Providing clarity around your expectations and processes makes doing the right thing easier. In *Cowboy Logic*, Ray Hunt writes, "Let your idea become the horse's idea." For what Ray suggests to take place, the cowboy's idea needs to be clear to the horse. Given a clear expectation and related encouragement, the horse will find comfort while coming to embrace the cowboy's idea as his own. We saw this in the example of Talmage and Apache, as the horse embraced a safe standing distance from humans and found a feeling of safety even away from the barn and other horses.

Given clear expectations and encouragement, your people will come to embrace your ideas, your visions, and your goals and objectives as their own. They will work to achieve consistent success in completing the tasks set before them.

PART II

EXPECTATIONS AT A GLANCE

CHAPTER 9:
WE ALL NEED CLEAR EXPECTATIONS
AND BOUNDARIES

1. Clearly communicated expectations are fundamental for effective supervision and leadership.

2. If an action isn't carried out within its boundaries, there must be consequences. Consequences make sure the decision, action, and any corresponding boundaries are real and meaningful.

CHAPTER 10:
ALL ATTEMPTS TO MEET NEEDS OR
FIX PROBLEMS RESULT IN UNINTENDED
CONSEQUENCES

3. By taking a little time, you can determine a number of different ways to approach a task or ways to resolve a difficulty.

4. Unintended consequences can adversely affect someone else or, in fact, can make the original problem worse.

5. To resolve the problem of unintended consequences, take the time to identify a number of alternative solutions or alternative tasks to meet a need before deciding on a plan of action. Then, use your imagination to determine potential unintended consequences for each alternative. Determine which unintended consequences you can best handle.

CHAPTER 11:
WE RESPOND TO ENCOURAGEMENT
AND REWARDS

6. The combination of firm but reassuring pressure and rewarding and comforting release leads to an atmosphere of encouragement and a foundation for building trust.

7. One significant way to reverse a difficult cycle of attitudes and behaviors between two people is through the associated attitude of encouragement.

8. Change often leads to stress; many times, stress leads to conflict.

CHAPTER 12:
IN A NEW WORLD, WE DO
THINGS DIFFERENTLY

9. The Theory X management approach represents the traditional view of direction and control.

10. The Theory Y management approach represents the more current view of supervision based on participation and support.

11. The Theory X and Theory Y approaches are essentially opposite in nature. If you take one approach, you can't take the other.

12. Theory X may work for a supervisor who believes in it. However, Theory Y has been shown to work much better for a broad spectrum of supervisors, especially in a global environment.

13. Manage and supervise for the best among your team members, rather than for the worst among them.

CHAPTER 13:
IT'S ABOUT CHANGE

14. Change is hard. Prepare and position your people for change.

15. Relatively speaking, people don't dislike change as much as they dislike other people trying to change them.

16. When asking for change, you're expecting people to carry out tactical and operational activities based on your strategy and vision. Setting goals, directions, and purposes are strategic activities. Determining and providing resources are tactical activities. Providing and implementing processes or procedures for using resources in achieving the goals are operational activities.

17. Ask several times. If you don't get the response to the change you need, then take the directing stance. If there's still no response, make the situation around the unwanted or unhelpful behavior uncomfortable.

18. People tend to tell most of the time, but they should be asking more.

19. Those for whom you're responsible want to know when you want their input (participative decision making and generating new ideas) and when you want their output ("head down, butt up, scratch dirt").

20. Supervisors need to share their thinking and take time to explain why each change (not just the what, but the so-what) is important, how and when each transition will be accomplished, and what the anticipated results of making the change are.

CHAPTER 14:
KNOW THE PROCESS

21. Supervisors need to know the appropriate methods to get the results they envision.

22. Because a process exists in an environment of changing constraints and new opportunities, it will need to be changed to adjust to the new constraints and to improve efficiency within the old constraints.

CHAPTER 15:
WHAT HAPPENED?

23. All events or results telegraph themselves.

24. Unattended nits (small problems) tend to become gnats (medium problems), and unattended gnats become tanks (disasters).

25. If you're attentive, you'll discover signs of a potential problem before the problem happens. The people closest to the action in the workplace know what's going on and what the difficulties are. If trust exists in the workplace, people will communicate their information to the leader.

CHAPTER 16:
WE PERFORM BEST WITH
COMFORT AND CLARITY

26. Clarity may be the biggest contributor to the peace and comfort of people (and horses).

27. Providing clarity about your expectations and how to proceed makes doing the right thing easier for others.

PART III

WE MANAGE THROUGH
BUILDING ENDURING
RELATIONSHIPS

INTRODUCTION

UNCLE JIM'S CHANGE OF HEART

TIM THAYNE: My rural upbringing was a family affair. I have rich memories of experiencing our ranch and horses with all my family members, but I'm particularly fond of my Uncle Jim. Uncle Jim, who stands at a stout 5'10", has a contagious, easy laugh and a most generous heart. On the farm, he's invaluable. As a handyman, he can build or fix anything with his thick, sausage-sized fingers. He also knows an awful lot about animals.

As far back as I can remember, Uncle Jim was known for his ability to make a friend out of anyone, animal or human. In his younger years, Uncle Jim naturally connected with animals. Horses, cats, and even some wild animals would readily, regularly approach him. Once he trained a deer; once he trained a hawk. Rather than having to chase animals to pet them, like the rest of us did, the same animals would gravitate to him.

One night, as Uncle Jim and I reminisced about our past and about how he had connected so easily with animals, he told me about the day a horse kicked him in the face. Uncle Jim prefaced the story by admitting he was going about his work with the horse that day in all the wrong ways. First of all, he said, he probably shouldn't have been working on a Sunday. However, he was in a hurry because he had to ride out to a far pasture and bring a salt block back to the cattle. As luck would have it, before he got to the cattle, his horse threw a shoe. A horse's shoeless hoof is easily injured, so Uncle Jim knew he needed to tend to the problem immediately. Since he didn't think he had time to return to the corral, he grabbed his toolbox and started to reshoe the horse right there in the field.

As Uncle Jim was diligently working, bent over his horse's foot, a frisky, naturally curious colt drifted over to see what was going on. Soon, the colt was nosing around the toolbox. Whenever Uncle Jim would shoo the colt away, the colt would whirl, jump, and playfully buck.

The third time, the colt got too close. Uncle Jim threw up both his arms and hollered at the colt. Quite spooked, the colt wheeled around and threw up his heels. Unfortunately, the colt's hoof caught Uncle Jim right in the face. At first, Uncle Jim jumped up angrily, ready to teach the colt a lesson. However, he quickly realized the colt had done nothing wrong. Uncle Jim and his face simply had been in the wrong place at the wrong time.

At first, Uncle Jim didn't know how badly hurt he was. However, when he leaned down to grab his hat, which had fallen off in the skirmish, he saw blood pouring from his face. Soon, he realized his nose had been almost completely knocked off and his glasses were broken. (As Uncle Jim recounted the tale, I remembered seeing him after the incident. His eyes were swollen shut and his face was all scraped up.)

Uncle Jim recalled, "I hit the colt's hoof with my nose. The colt wasn't at fault; I was. I spooked it. I should have been in less of a hurry and done things right. Naturally, a young colt would stick his nose in my business. What's more, I should have remembered the colt would also spook when I surprised it with my big voice and sudden movements."

"As a kid, I was so amazed by how animals came to you. I thought you were magic," I told Uncle Jim.

"I wasn't magic," he said. "I just had an open heart."

Later that same night, with sadness in his voice, Uncle Jim shared with me how some difficult life experiences, such as his painful divorce, had caused him to close that heart. He noted animals just didn't approach him the way they had in the past. He believed his natural connection with animals had disappeared.

"It was because I closed my heart," he said, with regret. "I got to a point and decided I wasn't going to let anything get close to me."

I listened intently.

"You can't trust any human, not women, and especially not weaselly guys. Still, I know I'm cheating the people I love in my life. They deserve and aren't getting my open heart. I keep my distance because I don't want to get hurt or to hurt others." At that point, he looked at me directly. "You know, Tim, I just couldn't do it anymore, and now I'm stuck. I'm impatient and short-tempered, but I just don't want to be hurt anymore."

I was saddened and surprised by Uncle Jim's deep anger and his matter-of-fact description of his current emotional state: his closed heart.

We continued to talk for a while.

Then, Uncle Jim recounted a terrible experience he'd had not too long beforehand. "One afternoon I took on a colt to train for its owner," he told me. "I saddled the colt with my brand-new, beautiful saddle, which I'd been working on for months. Oh, was I proud of my new saddle. I rode the colt out on the range and we came upon a ditch with flowing water. It was about three feet wide and the water about three feet deep.

"The long-legged colt – 17 hands high – seemed afraid of stepping through ditches with running water flowing in them. I didn't want the colt to try jumping every ditch he came to, so I decided he had to learn to step through flowing water, but with each attempt I made to encourage the colt to move into the water, the young horse balked. I got impatient. So, I made the mistake of deciding to put my 230-pound self against the rump of the 1,200-pound colt and push.

"My idea was to get the colt to step into the water. I hoped that once he got a hoof wet, the colt would realize the water wouldn't hurt him and he'd step on across the ditch. Boy, was that a mistake. The colt lost his footing and flipped over into the ditch, new saddle down. He was stuck in the ditch like a cork in a bottle, and very likely could have drowned. Of course, I jumped straight into the ditch. Using all the strength I could muster, I got the colt's head and shoulders up out of the water and prevented him from drowning."

Uncle Jim paused, looking down at his shoes with a deep sigh. "I made the colt afraid of running water. Forever. I don't think he will ever step into water again, and it's my fault – my impatience, my anger, my closed heart. I feel terrible about what I did to him. It's not what the water did or what the horse did; it's about what I did."

As a result, Uncle Jim said, he had become afraid of some horses.

Despite his acknowledgement of a closed heart, I knew then that my old Uncle Jim was still in there. He was able to recognize and admit the unfortunate experience was his fault, and he didn't blame the horse. Because of that, I thought Uncle Jim was on the mend.

That night, I couldn't stop thinking about Uncle Jim. I knew how sad he was. He loved his connection with animals and missed the jovial way with which he used to connect with people. However, because Uncle Jim was able to talk about his feelings, I was hopeful he would be able to turn his difficult situation around and find an open heart again. I thought the severity of the incident with the colt was the jolt he had needed. Now, he not only wanted an open heart again, but, more importantly, he realized he needed the open heart he'd once had.

Not long ago, Uncle Jim was out on the range with my oldest son, Mitchell, and a couple of other children. The alternator belt had come off the pulleys in Uncle Jim's diesel truck. No directions for how to rewind the serpentine belt were available in the truck. This made for a situation that could have led to frustration and impatience. Instead, Uncle Jim, who knew how to rewind the belt from his many years of experience on the farm, made the situation into a teaching opportunity and advised Mitchell step by step, rephrasing and repeating the directions for how the belt fit around the several pulleys involved, until my son was able to repair the truck.

When I picked Mitchell up afterwards, he eagerly told me about the wonderful time he'd had fixing the truck with Uncle Jim.

Knowing about Uncle Jim's struggle with feelings of impatience and a closed heart, I later asked him, "How did you show such patience at that difficult time? What did you draw on within yourself to help you do that?"

"Typically, as my closed-hearted self, I would've been irritated and gotten short and ornery," Uncle Jim said. "But, this time, I took a moment to draw on all those other times when I was impatient and remember all the bad results I ended up with. I didn't want bad results with Mitchell. So, I knew I had to deal with this situation differently."

All this shows that, slowly but surely, Uncle Jim's heart is opening again. When he remembers what happened when he was open and trusting before, Uncle Jim admits he's scared; he knows just how badly he can be hurt. In the end, though, Uncle Jim doesn't want to be bitter or distrustful. He's found a loss of innocence and trust seems to invite problems he didn't encounter before he closed his heart. Upon reflection, he's also found he doesn't have to be like a frightened colt in running water, afraid for the rest of his life. Now, Uncle Jim diligently searches for ways to create good experiences for himself and everyone around him again. He's discovered good experiences begin with a deliberate openness of the heart.

Recently, Uncle Jim told me about his friend, Pat Parelli, whose words have helped Uncle Jim so much. "Pat said he's improved his relationships with people by applying what he knows about horses to humans. The basic principle with horses is to get them to come to you, and Pat says it's just the same way with people."

Since Uncle Jim has more faith in horses' abilities to develop effective partnerships than in people's, he's begun to remember the exceptional moments he's had with horses, including those times when he gave horses the benefit of the doubt. Not long ago, he told me, "I'm learning to be as thankful for trials as I am for good fortune." Uncle Jim's patience and openness seem to be working, not only because horses and other animals are approaching him with ease once again, but also because he's remembering how to connect with people again. The awful encounter with the colt encouraged Uncle Jim to seek out his open heart; his desire to build a strong connection with Mitchell was the perfect opportunity to begin the reopening process.

Tim's story about Uncle Jim's change of heart has many lessons, which we'll discuss in the chapters noted in the parentheses:

1. Life's experiences offer opportunities to consider important questions. Here are some questions to consider, pertaining to Uncle Jim's experiences:

- Do you think Jim can ever get back to his innocent open heartedness?
- Is a deliberately open heart more helpful than an innocently open heart?
- Is a deliberately open heart more practical for a rancher?
- What kind of open heart is most helpful for Uncle Jim – and for you (Chapter 17)?

2. When you have an open heart, your facial expression, tone of voice, and body language make that openness obvious to others. Uncle Jim was an open book to all creatures (including humans), whether they had an open heart or a closed one (Chapter 17).

3. When Uncle Jim worked to reconnect with his past experiences, times when he had an open heart and when he was happy with the results of trusting animals naturally coming to him, he remembered exceptional moments. These moments were times when he succeeded in some way he didn't expect or accomplished something he thought he couldn't do. By reconnecting with his exceptional moments and recognizing what he had contributed to those situations, Uncle Jim discovered what he could do or think that would allow him to achieve those desirable results again (Chapter 18).

4. Uncle Jim recognized the youth, vivaciousness, and goodness inside the first colt, even though the animal kicked him in the face. Some might call what the colt did "bad behavior" (and that's probably true), but, through it all, Uncle Jim saw the goodness in that colt (Chapter 19).

5. Uncle Jim had the wisdom to realize that the colt was surprised and probably startled or threatened. The colt instinctively tried to get away from the situation, with disastrous results (Chapter 20).

6. Ultimately, each of us needs to know who he or she really is. Uncle Jim has been and is going through changes in how he

presents himself to the world. After reading the story, we're left wondering whether Uncle Jim will discover if his real self is the one with an open heart. Perhaps he'll discover the closed heart was a façade he used to protect himself (Chapter 21).

7. To feel complete, Uncle Jim recognizes he must get back to the person he is when he has an open heart. While children with an open heart tend to spontaneously exhibit their openness, Uncle Jim knows he needs to be more deliberate than spontaneous. That way, he can recapture what he's lost (Chapter 21).

8. While people may not look fragile, to a greater or lesser extent, all of them are fragile inside. Uncle Jim opened his heart wide and was vulnerable to the blows life tends to hand each of us. Unprepared and unable to deal with the ways in which others exploited and abused his open-heartedness, Uncle Jim was crushed by hurtful experiences (Chapter 22).

9. Uncle Jim's attitude and feelings affected others around him, even animals (Chapter 23).

10. When Uncle Jim's heart was closed to others, he demonstrated thoughts and behaviors that revealed his indifference. Contrary to what many people assume or think, the opposite of love isn't necessarily hate. Instead, the opposite of love is "not love." Part of "not love" is not caring, and not caring translates to indifference. Uncle Jim's pain led to him being indifferent to the world and, generally, to those around him.

Animals read the signs of Uncle Jim's indifference and avoided him; they no longer felt safe around him (Chapter 24).

11. After considering Uncle Jim's efforts to return to an open heart, we realize his new open heart is *deliberate.* This time around, his open heart is more thinking-based or analytical, not feeling-based or intuitive. Now, Uncle Jim must work to retrain his heart, hoping he'll be more instinctive once again (Chapter 24).

12. Uncle Jim's closed heart resulted in anger, impatience, and fear, all of which led to indifference. To regain his open heart, Uncle Jim had and has to turn away from indifference and learn to care again (Chapter 24).

13. There should be no barriers to the learning process. Uncle Jim found if he had the right type of relationship with a horse, that horse learned twice as fast. Conversely, if you correct a horse while you're frustrated and angry, the horse's natural instincts for self-preservation take over and the learning process stops. A horse can't think about and feel two things at once. A horse won't sense frustration and anxiety while also wanting to draw nearer to the cowboy ("Final Thoughts").

14. During the time Uncle Jim's heart was open, animals were drawn to him. Everywhere he went, he made animals feel safe, comfortable, confident, and welcome ("Final Thoughts").

In Your Workplace ...

The principles and practices illustrated through the story of Uncle Jim give us an engaging entry to Part III ("We Manage through Building Enduring *Relationships*"), in which we discuss the importance of promoting trust and leading with an open heart. The organization of the following chapters is based upon a progression of thought:

- You lead by loving the people for whom you're responsible. In the workplace, to love is to accurately assess and adequately meet another person's needs. When people are valued, appreciated, respected, and understood, they're in a safe environment in which they can best empower themselves to display their unique strengths (Chapter 17).
- You focus on what people do right and help them reflect on what they do right so they can continually bring their strengths and effort to situations (Chapter 18).
- You believe each person wants to do the best he or she can do. If you maintain the position of believing in your people, enduring relationships will flourish (Chapter 19).
- You provide people with consistency, which provides comfort. You also allow people processing time and space in which to work, which supports trust (Chapter 20).
- You lead by example, so lead with kindness and generosity. Understand your own strengths, biases, and perspectives so you are able to be other-focused as you lead (Chapter 21).
- You are clear, consistent, and focused in your leadership. When people feel safe, trust thrives. A leader wants trust in the workplace (Chapter 22).
- You nurture people's creativity and intuition. You develop

an environment that provides people with the information, materials, and time they need to be creative (Chapter 23).

- You communicate your expectations of caring because there's no greater empowering idea than that of people who believe they matter to other people. Therefore, you must learn about the people you work with and their work (Chapter 24).

- You develop an environment in which people can learn, grow, and contribute ("Final Thoughts").

CHAPTER 17

YOU CAN'T HIDE THE CONDITION OF YOUR HEART

A horse will know an open heart when it sees one.

---

horse will know an open heart when it sees one. As we learned from Uncle Jim's experience, a horse can sense an open heart and will gravitate to a person with an open heart. People may not be as good as horses are at recognizing others' open hearts, but humans too will gravitate to other people who have what they sense are open hearts. In his early years, Uncle Jim's unconditionally open heart brought him (and those around him) great joy. Yet Uncle Jim's open heart also got him into trouble in his personal life. If you have an open heart, you're vulnerable to being hurt. Therefore, as Uncle Jim's experience demonstrates, people will counter the hurt they experience by developing defense mechanisms they can use to protect themselves. Once he began recognizing what he was missing with a closed heart, Uncle Jim decided he wanted to regain an open heart. At that stage, Uncle Jim learned he had to develop an open heart deliberately. He no longer had the ability to be spontaneous.

How can we expand on this idea of open-heartedness in the workplace? We want to start with a piece of wisdom from Harold's pastor, John Yates, who says, "If you try to lead them without loving them, you'll fail them." When Harold first heard this statement, he was struck with how significant the idea could be for leaders.

To explore this idea further, let's define the concept of *love* in the workplace: to love is to accurately assess and adequately meet another person's needs. For love among family members, we'll adjust the definition by changing two words: to love is to accurately assess and abundantly satisfy another person's needs. Why change the definition to apply to each of these contexts? Meeting needs in the workplace is more *contractual* ("adequately meet"), while satisfying needs in the family is more *covenantal* ("abundantly satisfy").

To expand, in the workplace, leaders (executives, project managers, support personnel, and supervisors) must meet the needs of internal and external clients (peers, direct reports, other supervisors, and so forth). Leaders have to be careful about going too far beyond a contract with clients in meeting needs. They have to make sure they meet a client's needs without overdoing it. Therefore, in our definition, we use "adequately meet." Leaders must ensure they supply what the contract calls for, and maybe a bit more. For instance, if you determine a client needs greater effort and results than a contract or work statement dictates, you need to develop a new contract or work statement. If the client doesn't agree with the different contractual needs, your responsibility is to meet those needs as defined in the existing (and reviewed) contract. The difference between *adequate* and *abundant* is subtle but important in the business world. If leaders don't understand the difference, their organizations will go out of business.

Love among family members is quite different from obligations expressed in a business contract. A covenant, which is written, in a sense, on the heart, goes beyond what anyone can put on paper. With family members, you may satisfy a person's need for excess, as in harvesting an abundant crop on the family farm or ranch. The idea of "satisfying" a family member's need means fulfilling the family member's needs, expectations, wishes, or desires. In this context, *satisfy* is more like *gratify*. In contrast, workplace leaders need to meet the client's needs to comply with or complete the requirements of the contractual agreement. Again, the subtle difference between meeting needs and satisfying needs is important.

To sum up, in business, where leaders need to be more careful about putting themselves in vulnerable positions, they should present deliberate, controlled open hearts; at home, where family members share history, culture, and dreams, they should strive for more unconditionally open hearts.

The differences described above are less significant overall because both definitions lead people to be other-focused. When people are other-focused, they put aside their selfishness and open their minds and hearts. At that point, they're able to read the subtleties of others' needs and care enough to find a way to meet or satisfy those needs.

Significantly, in family-type relationships, people can read those needs at a deeper level; sometimes, people can access a level so deep that the other person hasn't yet crystallized it in his or her mind.

Love, at home and in business, is other-focused. The accurate assessment of a client's need requires businesspeople to focus on the client. Leaders don't focus on what *they* want to do or what *they* have to offer. Instead, they focus on what the client needs. Meeting the need adequately requires being responsive to the client: carrying out other-focus through actions or offerings geared to *fit the client's need*.

Subconsciously, people have a universal set of needs underlying their momentary needs. What do those people need from their leaders to be productive and satisfied in their work? They need these simple things:

- **To be valued.** 70 percent of people who leave jobs do so because they feel they don't matter.
- **To be appreciated.** Knowing you're appreciated builds self-confidence and self worth.
- **To be respected.** When a person feels respected, he or she will excel.
- **To be understood.** People can be quick to find fault, but learning what a person feels and needs takes time.
- **To be safe.** People don't want others to take advantage of them.

If people feel valued, appreciated, respected, understood, and safe, they will participate in an environment in which they can best empower themselves and display their unique strengths and resources.

According to systems theory, a group of people who spend time together will develop a shared emotional system. This theory has two primary principles:

1. Whatever affects one person in the system emotionally affects all the others in the system. Emotions move easily from person to person in the group.
2. People in a group tend to connect rather tightly. They trade fundamental parts of themselves back and forth.

You can observe the movement of emotion through a group, which can be as small as two individuals: two people or a cowboy and his horse.

The Bowen theory (named after Murray Bowen, a leader in family systems therapy) states this flow of emotion within a group is subconscious and based on the more primitive parts of the brain, primarily the part called the mammalian brain. The next time you take a Sunday drive in the country, use that thought as you observe the horses. Suppose you come across two groups of horses, one group in a field on one side of the road and another group in a field on the other side. If something agitates one horse, soon the agitation will spread throughout that horse's group. While the horses across the road may become aware of the agitation, they don't get caught up in it because they aren't part of the emotional system across the road. They may show some curiosity, but they will continue in their original emotional state. Similarly, people can't help being influenced by the moods and emotions of those closest to them. The passing of emotion is instinctive, and just as horses pass agitation within their groups, people pass agitation in the workplace.

Like so many people living in response to painful experiences, Uncle Jim protected himself from being injured again in different ways. His ability to love and trust without barriers had been damaged, and his connection to animals was impaired. He'd lost his attractiveness to animals. Why are people's relationships with others, horses or people, impaired when they've been hurt? What messages might a hurt person send out to others, skewing or even blocking relationships with them? People display changes in their energy; they can demonstrate defensive body language, a release of hormones, or both. Every minute of the day, people are projecting seen and unseen information about themselves to be interpreted by those around them.

A horse will pick up emotion in a cowboy through the saddle, reins, and air. An effective cowboy has an intimate physical connection with his horse. Each cowboy influences whether his horse is energetic, ready, willing, and eager, or apathetic, disinterested, and spiritless. If the cowboy is calm, the horse will tend to be calm. If the cowboy is anxious, the horse will tend to be anxious. In the workplace, you can observe how each person influences the group through body language and tone of voice (not physical touch).

HORSE SENSE
If the cowboy is calm, the horse will tend to be calm.

Jay Brewer tells a story about one of his workers. The man had issues in his personal life that came out as anger when he was working with horses. Whenever this man came into the barn, the horses would raise their heads and watch him, sensing the negative energy, and either stay put or move away. In contrast, when a cowboy enters a barn, natural horse trainers want the horses to look up with interest and eagerness, so they connect with that cowboy. For this attitude to prevail, a trainer needs to be aware of his emotional state when connecting with a horse, which is a good idea for supervisors in the workplace as well.

In sending and receiving oral messages effectively – oral messages are sent through speaking and received by listening – people "listen" more with their eyes than with their ears. People listen with their ears for words and tone of voice, and they "listen" through their eyes for body language and facial expression (see Chapter 3).

In any group, there are pivotal people who influence the remaining members. These pivotal people aren't necessarily those in positions of power. Next time you're in a meeting, watch for the influence such a person has on the group. If one person looks at a discussion topic or situation through a lens of hope and excitement, the rest of the group will tend to pick up on those emotions until another person interrupts the flow with a more depressing view. One person can infuse joy and optimism into the entire group, while another person can put a damper on the whole thing. While you're obviously not the only influence on a group, you can choose what *kind* of influence you want to be. Which type of person, in your opinion, is most helpful?

Humans read each other's mental and emotional states in the workplace by noticing body language and tone of voice, just as a horse senses a cowboy's mental and emotional state through physical contact. In *Think Harmony with Horses*, Ray Hunt explains, "If the rider is alert and aware and in a learning frame of mind, the horse can be the same." Not only does the horse read the cowboy's state, but the horse also mimics the cowboy's state. The cowboy's state is contagious. Ray offers the terms *feel, timing,* and *balance* as the keys to achieving harmony with a horse. He believes people need a lifetime of learning to understand the terms completely. However, people achieve harmony in a number of ways, some of which are instinctive. Both cowboys and supervisors should want to be alert purposefully, since an alert frame of mind will affect those around them.

Recognizing each person is unique and responds better to different methods of treatment, it seems clear that people tend to perform best when they have the right amount of emotion, or balance, in their work. Louis Wood emphasizes the importance of balance in a cowboy and horse's setting: "You want to help the horse stay in balance. When pressure leads toward imbalance, the horse gets frightened." Balance is important in everything: between life and work, between quality and quantity, and between pressure to produce and recognition of effort. Balance applies to perspective and to physical stability. When people (or horses) are bored or disinterested, they don't perform well. When they are panicky or agitated, they don't perform well. However, when they're alert, enthused, calm, positive, and confident, they perform best. Whatever that behavior turns out to be, it can influence others too.

In other words, individuals' emotions are contagious. Emotion spreads through a group like an epidemic. The good news is people get to choose whether they will contribute to an epidemic of comfort and excitement, boredom and disinterest, or panic and agitation. Louis Wood says that the level of such an epidemic is in direct proportion to one's "life." The energy (that is, the degree) and type (the feeling of comfort, boredom, agitation, and so on) of life in a horse, or in others in the workplace, reflects the energy and type of life in the cowboy, or workplace leaders. In other words, leaders' role modeling relates to work ethic, attitude, maturity, and more. What leaders role model is contagious. So, in the workplace, often leaders must deliberately interject helpful attitudes and feelings of optimism into situations. We believe you can act your way into more helpful ways of thinking. We also believe you can act and think your way into more helpful ways of feeling.

To be effective supervisors, leaders need to have intimate mental connections with the people for whom they're responsible. They also need to have appropriate emotional connections. Simply put, direct reports and other subordinates pick up on leaders' thoughts and emotions. So, while leaders often send signals about their thoughts with purpose, they also tend to send signals about their emotions without realizing it. Therefore, leaders must be very cognizant of themselves and their behavior. This somewhat frightening thought leads to the understanding of a basic premise in management and leadership. Leaders need to assess, evaluate, understand, and supervise themselves. In other words, they need to cultivate personal mastery, a quality good leaders have in abundance.

In *The Heart of Leadership*, Dusty Staub identifies four chambers in, as stated in the book's title, the heart of leadership: competence, integrity, intimacy, and passion. The kind of intimacy mentioned in the third chamber has to do with the concept of profound knowledge, an idea espoused by W. Edwards Deming in his discussion of total quality management. To achieve a significant level of quality and performance, we need profound knowledge of the work, profound knowledge of the client, and profound knowledge of those we work with. Staub explains, "Without intimacy there exists only superficial contact, only token leadership."

To review, in the workplace, how do you develop and share an open heart?

An open heart is other-focused, a concept we've discussed throughout this book (specifically in Chapters 1, 2, 3, and 6). The more people move out of their own concerns, hurts, and issues, the more they're open to the needs of others. In other words, the more they care. Revealing your open heart to someone else implies trust in and eagerness to learn about and from that other person. As you focus on opening your heart, try these strategies:

1. Count the number of times a day you say to yourself, "I don't trust that person or situation."
2. Wonder what another person is thinking or feeling. If needed, ask him or her about those thoughts or feelings. Present your question with a sense of caring.
3. Ask yourself what you're thinking or feeling about another person or a situation.

The answers to these questions will tell you a great deal about whether your heart is open or closed.

CHAPTER 18

WE CHANGE THROUGH OUR
EXCEPTIONAL MOMENTS

Give a horse time to reflect on how
it got somewhere, especially when it does
something right.

---

ive a horse time to reflect on how it got somewhere, especially when it does something right. In working with horses or with people, you can choose to focus on a glass that's half-empty or a glass that's half-full. People who believe their contribution to the world is in solving problems tend to focus on the half-empty glass, or the problem.

Otherwise, there's nothing left to fix. The principle discussed in this chapter, however, implies the preferred life approach is to focus on the glass as half-full. However, focusing on a glass as being half-full doesn't mean you have to ignore the fact the glass is also half-empty. This is a matter of focus. Ultimately, it's also a matter of *exceptional moments*.

Any person will have times in life when he or she does something better than at other times. These times are exceptional moments. A leader focuses on exceptional moments and helps other people focus on them too. An exceptional moment doesn't have to be a time when a person excels at a task. Instead, the exceptional moment is when the person does the task *better than usual*. During such exceptional moments, people bring their strengths to their tasks in helpful ways. When you help someone recognize those strengths and how he or she contributed to the more successful accomplishment, the person can use those strengths again, later on, in a more purposeful way.

Good leaders want people to reflect on their experiences in order to learn from what they said, did, or decided. Reflecting on experience takes introspection, something most people haven't perfected. Introspection is improved with help, though, and other people provide that help. If leaders focus on the glass half-empty, or what subordinates did wrong, they solidify unhelpful attitudes and behaviors that lead to less-than-helpful results. Instead, leaders should focus on what other people do right, thereby solidifying more helpful attitudes and behaviors. Some people, typically the pessimists among us, more naturally see the glass as half-empty while other, more optimistic people are inclined to see the glass as half-full. Helping those not otherwise inclined to look at the half-full scenario changes their focus. This is how leaders begin to support the people they work with to think favorably about their performance and abilities, thus motivating the subordinates to do better. Sometimes, leaders can seek help from those around them who see the glass half-full to help change their (the leaders') perspective.

When Harold works with organizations, he uses a special technique to help people escalate exceptional moments into new strengths. To implement this technique, Harold relies on little round plastic tokens, which are a little more than an inch in diameter, imprinted with the words, "I did it well that time." The technique relies on the fact people will have exceptional moments. To start taking advantage of the technique, people must identify a behavior they want to improve. For example, they may know they tell more than ask, and they want to do better at asking as opposed to telling. Using about five tokens each morning, they place the five tokens in a particular spot, perhaps in a pocket or on a desk. Each time they catch themselves performing the new behavior (or at least making a thoughtful effort), they move one token to a different spot.

As they focus on recognizing and purposefully producing exceptional moments, they find more and more opportunities to acknowledge or act using new, desired behaviors. After about a month of using the technique, they recognize they are behaving differently. They feel successful for doing the right thing and don't worry whenever they don't do the right thing. The technique's objective is to encourage people to move the tokens, which indicates they are focusing on exceptional moments. In other words, this technique teaches people to see the glass as half-full.

These tokens represent the concept of accumulating small successes to achieve big successes. For instance, one experience of asking, instead of telling, leads to another asking experience. Over time, these experiences lead to a new mindset of learning (not judging) and being other-focused. To turn to another example, as

Uncle Jim moves forward by recalling his many exceptional moments in which he opened his heart and achieved results he liked, he can regain his open-heart demeanor by considering the strengths he drew upon early in life to maintain that open heart.

However, not all people can recognize the exceptional times in their lives when they had an opportunity to do something well, especially if the activity was something they don't typically do well. For Uncle Jim, recalling when he had been impatient, along with the distaste he developed for the consequences of his impatience, persuaded him to be more patient. In this case, Uncle Jim was able to use an unfavorable exceptional moment to help himself do better in returning to the person he wanted to be.

Consider this additional principle from Louis Wood: "If you get the feeling you can't do *anything* right, you want to leave the relationship." Louis is talking about a horse leaving the horse-cowboy relationship. However, his principle applies across the board in the workplace. When people feel they can't do anything right, they'll consider emotionally or physically leaving their relationship with the supervisor, work team, or organization.

HORSE SENSE
"Make the wrong thing difficult and the right thing easy."
– Ray Hunt

Leaders don't want to focus on what others do wrong. If they do, sooner or later those others will quit their relationships with the leaders (either physically or emotionally). In any case, the result is you no longer have a relationship or a work team. So, leaders must focus on what others do right; they must focus on people's strengths. In this way, leaders can remain connected with those people.

Should leaders ignore what people do incorrectly? Of course not. Leaders don't focus solely on errors. As the principle of this chapter suggests, individuals want to leave relationships when they get the feeling they can't do anything right. To prevent this, first identify where individuals are and what they do right. Focus your attention, and, if possible, the delegated work assignments, on where they show their strengths. Then, model, teach, and reinforce additional efforts so they can expand and add to what they do right.

Still, be careful. In the case of particular people, you might be thinking you've identified many things they don't do right and only one or two things they do right. Don't send these people the message they do everything wrong. As it is, they will feel as though they can't do anything right if you don't manage the conversation appropriately – that is, if the one or two things you've identified as good either aren't the conversation's focus or are seemingly insignificant when compared to the list of things not done right. Naturally, if they feel as though they can't do anything right, and are thereby not helpfully contributing to the project or team's success, they will want out of the relationship with you, the work team, and/or the organization.

So, as a leader, what can you do to deal with people who have trouble doing things right? In *Think Harmony with Horses*, Ray Hunt explains, "Make the wrong thing difficult and the right thing easy ... Admire the horse for the good things he does and just *kinda* ignore the wrong things. First thing you know, the good things will get better and the bad things will get less." (As we discussed in Chapter 7, you get what you focus on.)

As a supervisor and leader, your job is to fix things so correct behavior is the easiest thing to do and wrong behavior the hardest thing. The easiest way to achieve this is to focus on what you want from those who work for you. Appreciate their good efforts. We believe you shouldn't ignore when people do something wrong. Perhaps you "just kinda ignore" them, as Hunt wrote. So, don't focus on what isn't helpful. Address those things, but don't focus on them, because you get what you focus on.

What's the right way to do something, anyhow? As a supervisor, when you're successful at work, you assume the right way is the way you followed, the way that allowed you to be successful. However, people all have different strengths, resources, and experiences. Therefore, what's the right way for one person may not be the right way for others. Usually, the other person can't be successful in the same way the original person was successful. Significantly, most people tend to believe the way they were successful at something is *the* way. Of course, there are other ways and, as a leader, your job is to help your people discover their own ways of being successful. A good leader helps people become successful in their own way by helping them reflect on what they do right and what they bring to the table when they do well.

Here's what we believe is the universal truth on this topic, as expressed by Ray Hunt in *Think Harmony with Horses*: "When you ask your horse to do something, it should be his idea. This is the goal. In the end, when you ask your horse to do something, he wants to do it, he likes to do it, he understands how to do it, and he does it." In other words, the horse accomplishes the task his way. The supervisor (the cowboy) chooses the vision; the horse uses his strengths to accomplish the task leading toward that vision.

Expanding on his comment, Ray explains, "For me, the horse doesn't have to do my thing my way, but I do want him to do my thing his way and like it." That's a profound statement. In the workplace, you want people to follow your leadership and like it – a worthy goal.

CHAPTER 19
THERE'S A GOOD PERSON IN THERE!

Inside every horse is a good horse.

Inside every horse is a good horse. Similarly, there's a *good* person inside every person in your life. To understand this point, we have to determine the definition of good and decide whether we do, in fact, mean every person.

In most difficult confrontations, individuals assign blame to another person's actions, believing they know the other party's intent.

That leads to trouble. No one knows why another person says, does, or decides something. People can't read minds or know hearts. Yet, because people are taught that results are caused, they believe they can't improve results unless they deal with causes. Because of this attitude, people end up wasting time trying to guess at causes and, typically, dealing with wrong guesses.

We all receive sensory data – that is, information based on sound, sight, smell, taste, and touch – about incidents over time and relate this sensory data to our frames of reference (mental models, paradigms, and filters), generating thoughts in the conscious brain and feelings in the subconscious. So, when we speak, act, or decide something, we do so based on our thoughts and feelings. As our feelings give energy to our thoughts, we act, speak, or decide.

What does *good* mean? As we define the term here, a good person is someone who doesn't intentionally do harm. People can inadvertently do harm in several ways:

- People may try to protect themselves by lying.
- People may make mistakes.
- People may say or do something harmful or hurtful to others.
- Finally, people may be unaware of the consequences of their words or actions.

It's hard to find someone who hasn't committed at least one of these minor sins. It's also hard to determine, in some cases, whether the harm is inadvertent or purposeful. People may think there's intrigue when the situation was really caused by ignorance. Others may think someone means harm when, in reality, that person just doesn't know how to behave.

After doing hundreds of in-depth workshops with people, as well as a fair amount of executive coaching, we've found most people just want to get through the day as best they can. In our experience, which includes using techniques to help us "see inside" people, we usually find that someone who appears mean-spirited is trying to protect him- or herself. In other words, we find a good person inside the mean-spirited person.

Returning to the context of the horse and cowboy, Monty Roberts stresses the importance of understanding a horse's natural instincts in his book, *The Man Who Listens to Horses*. He emphasizes the horse's flight response when it is faced with potential danger: "The flight animal wants only to reproduce and survive; fear is the tool that allows him to survive. This has to be respected in any dealings with a horse, or he will be misunderstood ... The only way [to gain a horse's willing cooperation] is to earn the trust of the horse and never abuse his status as a flight animal." (We discuss the differences between fight, flight, and freeze animals in Chapter 22.)

This chapter's illustration shows a horse in the same circumstance humans often find themselves in: torn between goodness and "not-so-goodness." Horses have a herding instinct; an individual horse would rather go back to the barn and hang out with his friends. Many workplace subordinates would rather chat with their friends or check out the Internet than focus on their tasks. We believe approaching people from a position of wanting to contribute and do a good job will encourage the good people inside others to prevail. First, however, we have to believe there are good people in there. Second, we have to believe these people want to exhibit that "goodness." Once supervisors believe these two ideas, they can build effective relationships with those who work for them.

In Harold's work with many people, he has found that those who appear the most difficult, demanding, and harsh on the outside tend to be the softest, sweetest, and most sensitive on the inside. The problem for sweet and sensitive people is they get hurt easily. To protect themselves, they put up barriers; they close down and erect defenses. Sometimes, they even attack. Who said the best defense is a good offense?

Of course, one barrier or one defense doesn't do the trick. So, people put up more defenses. Over time, people can create so many barriers that their real selves become lost inside. Yet, deep inside each individual remains a good person. If you try hard and long enough, you'll probably catch a glimpse of that good person. That glimpse may change the way you see and deal with that individual. Yet do you really need that glimpse? You may be waiting for quite a while before you stumble on it.

Instead, wouldn't it just be easier to expect there's a good person inside each individual to begin with? There's a difference between expecting there's a good internal person and bringing that good person out. Bringing out a good person may take more time and effort than leaders can afford, given the many other people and tasks for which they are responsible. However, you might be surprised at the effect you have on others just by expecting there's a good individual inside each person you encounter. Remember, your expectations affect your demeanor, while your demeanor can affect others.

Based on the story at the beginning of Part III, we know Uncle Jim is a good person with a big heart. In his younger days, animals recognized his open heart and gravitated to him. He could train and work with animals easily. Yet, as we know, Uncle Jim got hurt, so he put up barriers and defenses to protect himself from more hurt. The animals couldn't understand Jim's painful experiences, but they

could recognize his closed heart. As a result, he couldn't train and work with animals the same way he once had. Horses can't always understand a person has been hurt, but other people can. People can give others a bit of leeway, especially after having a chance to glimpse through a crack in the hurt individual's façade. When Uncle Jim wanted to regain his open heart, he began by remembering there was a good person inside himself, just as there's a good horse inside every horse. Uncle Jim knew that principle to be true, even when he put his face in front of the colt's hoof.

HORSE SENSE

Horses can't always understand a person has been hurt,
but other people can.

It's wonderful to see someone crack a barrier or defense a bit, exposing the individual inside. Unfortunately, you don't always get the opportunity to see inside other people. So, what do you do then? We believe the best answer is to reverse the thinking. When someone appears "bad," you might think, "He's protecting himself." After all, haven't all of us been metaphorically kicked in the face, either in the workplace or in life?

More importantly, how do we deal with these painful experiences? Uncle Jim, like many other people we know, closed his heart because of the hurtful experiences he had with humans. He closed his heart because he believed he couldn't bear to be hurt again – and Uncle Jim assumed his heart inevitably would be hurt again. Because most people, like Uncle Jim, are just trying to protect themselves, there's no value or productivity in blaming them or retaliating against them.

Of course, not all people are good. There might always be a few bad apples, but we believe there are relatively few bad apples. We believe people shouldn't manage themselves or their work based on the worst among any group. Instead, we try to operate based on good faith in the best among us.

Remember Harold's personal rule, which was referenced in a previous chapter: "Everything I do to keep shirkers from shirking keeps producers from producing; everything I do to help producers produce helps shirkers shirk." In this scenario, you get to choose. Do you choose to help the producers produce, or do you choose to keep the shirkers from shirking? We choose to help the producers produce.

The theory behind the issue we describe here matches and recalls the difference between the Theory X and Theory Y approaches to supervision (discussed in depth in Chapter 12). Leaders who follow the Theory X approach assume people aren't to be trusted, need to be coerced to do a good job, and need to be punished for not doing a good job. Leaders who follow the Theory Y approach assume people want to do a good job and will do a good job if given the opportunity. Some supervisees may respond more readily to Theory X supervision and others may more readily respond to Theory Y. In today's world, because supervisees have ready access to information and want to participate in decision making, we believe leaders are better served by and deal with most people appropriately through the Theory Y approach.

Harold was once affiliated with a particular organization that had a community supply closet. He found that, from time to time, people would take supplies from the closet to use at home. Apparently, shirkers would take materials home to their families or give them to friends. Sometimes executive meetings would include discussions about the sins of inappropriately taking materials from the supply closet. Some supervisors wanted to lock the supply closet and have a closet guardian with a key. Others wanted to keep the closet unlocked all the time, regardless of what happened to the materials. In other words, one group wanted to keep the shirkers from shirking. The other group wanted to help the producers produce.

Harold was in the group that wanted to support the producers. He believed, and continues to do so, that if a person worked late or on the weekend and couldn't get the supplies he or she needed, the company might lose a motivated and productive worker. Keeping some from misbehaving leads to many feeling as though they're being told they can't be trusted. As the boss, Harold had the final say on this policy. He assumed good faith, so the closet door remained unlocked all the time.

A supervisor's job is to help the producers produce and to supply useful data, materials, and information to people in the organization. Harold wrote memos to briefly communicate the supply-and-demand data of the supply closet. Right after he sent out the memo, the closet behavior improved. Over time, the good behavior deteriorated. What did this mean? Time for another memo. In this scenario, the people who misused the supply closet were not necessarily crooks. Harold considers himself to be a good and honest person, certainly not a shirker. Yet even he has been known to find a U.S. Government-issue ballpoint pen at home.

In short, try to believe people are innately good and look for the good in others; that way, working relationships will develop and thrive.

CHAPTER 20

HELPFUL FEELINGS CONTRIBUTE TO PRODUCTIVE WORKPLACES AND HARMONIOUS RELATIONSHIPS

Your want your horse to make good decisions based on confidence and trust.

Y ou want your horse to make good decisions based on confidence and trust. To understand this principle, in this chapter we address two important questions:

1) How can you keep fear and anxiety away from what people have to do in the workplace?
2) How does an environment of fear and anxiety affect people's decisions?

Fear and anxiety are antithetical to security, confidence, and trust. You'll make entirely different decisions based on fear and anxiety than you will on confidence and trust. Which of those decisions do you believe are the most helpful?

For workers to make good decisions, supervisors should create an environment conducive to learning. In turn, learning contributes to an environment that supports trust, and when trust is present, workers (and supervisors) make better decisions, leading to effective actions.

Some years ago, Harold took a course and was surprised when, on the first day of class, the teacher said, "You all have an A." We'll bet you join us in wishing we all had more teachers like this one, who made a common practice of giving great grades out at the beginning of the course. We find the reason the teacher gave for this practice fascinating. She explained people practice a skill or attitude in the same mental state in which they learn the skill or attitude. If they learn a skill in a state of anxiety, they'll feel anxious when they use the skill. If they learn an attitude in a state of fear, they'll be afraid when they use the attitude. If they learn a skill in a state of self-confidence and trust, they'll be self-confident and trusting when they use the skill.

Giving an A to all students from the very beginning of a course isn't a unique idea, of course. In their book *The Art of Possibility*, Ben and Rosamund Zander include a chapter on "Giving an A." Ben, a professor at the New England Conservatory of Music, has a practice of giving an A to each of his students when courses begin. The A isn't a gift, but a possibility. Ben explains, "This A is not an expectation to live up to, but a possibility to live into." His students have "one requirement" they must fulfill to earn that grade. At the beginning of the course, they must write a letter (dated from the course's conclusion) telling Ben why they deserve the grade. Ben explains to students, "In this letter you are to tell, in as much detail as you can, the story of what will have happened to you by next May [the end of the course] that is in line with this extraordinary grade." In writing their letters, the students are setting expectations for themselves that go far beyond just a letter grade. These expectations lead to a helpful outlook on life and motivation in the workplace.

Consider the following questions:

- How can you establish situations in the workplace in which people feel they want to do what you need, in partnership with you?
- How can you help people set extraordinary expectations for themselves and feel confident in meeting those expectations?
- How can you motivate people to work productively while remaining in a mental state that supports both productivity and joy of workmanship through the joy of ownership (that is, through ownership of the work and the expectation)?
- How will partnerships of motivation and joy contribute to extraordinary relationships among people in the workplace?

In *True Horsemanship through Feel*, Bill Dorrance writes:

> The horse needs to have the person feeling real sure
> about how to present what is expected of him in a way he can
> understand. The horse can get sort of lost if he doesn't under-
> stand what's expected and he needs to learn what's expected
> of him way down at the bottom, through feel. What fits me
> best, in terms of helping someone out, is to help [him or her]
> get the feel of the horse and teach that horse [the] feel of
> [him or her].

Horses are different from the people you work with, right? Not in all ways. We don't believe horses have logic, but they do make choices. Making choices means making decisions. A cowboy influences those choices through training and through being connected with a horse in the moment. In *Think Harmony with Horses*, Ray Hunt advises riders, explaining, "In your own mind you have to have a picture of what you want from the horse, but you are the leader and you can ask him to follow you, just like dancing. It's a rhythm, a harmony…" As discussed in a previous chapter, this partnership we're looking for, either between cowboy and horse or between supervisor and subordinate, is similar to dancing.

In the illustration that accompanies this chapter, the cowboy and the horse are in sync. They're moving in harmony according to the pattern of their dance. They both know the steps of that dance and enjoy following those steps. So, whether you're working with horses or with subordinates, think about harmony. Life is much more enjoyable with harmony.

Over time, unless a cowboy is especially in tune with himself and his horse, he may lead the partnership into a mutually destructive

cycle of anger (on his part) and flighty self-preserving behaviors (on the horse's part). When this cycle appears, you can bet there's a basic problem with the cowboy's view of the horse. Anger usually comes from a selfish, ego-based perspective in which the other person's perspective is forgotten and the angry person thinks only of what he or she wants. Rather than seeing the horse as an individual with accompanying emotions, instincts, and personality to consider, he or she sees it as, simply, a vehicle. The partnership is really a supervisor/subordinate relationship, an idea the horse will soon figure out.

To this day, Uncle Jim is sad about some of the consequences of his actions with the colt he forced into the ditch. Not only did he almost drown, the colt never lost his fear of water. In fact, Uncle Jim never got the colt to step into water again. Uncle Jim knew his impatience and closed heart got in the way of the colt's development. As a result, the animal was never trained as well as Uncle Jim wanted, nor as well as the colt could and should have been trained. As for that brand-new, beautiful leather saddle? Unfortunately for Uncle Jim, the time and money he spent on obtaining the saddle was, for the most part, wasted: the saddle was never the same after being submerged in that ditch. In this story, Uncle Jim and the colt didn't have a successful dance.

Have you ever had a work relationship that felt more like dancing, when you understood what the other person was thinking, needed, or was planning to do? In such a relationship, the parties don't use words or obvious signals; they rely on an instinctive understanding. Authors Tim and Harold enjoy this kind of harmonious relationship. When they're giving leadership workshops, one of them always knows what the other needs, when to chime in, when to hold back, and when to take charge. This kind of rhythm or harmony leads to more than productivity. Their relationship helps them make seamless contributions to their shared goals, as they help each other make better efforts and ideas, which leads to them exceeding their expectations. In discussing this kind of harmonious relationship between cowboy and horse, Ray Hunt advises, "You can't make any of this happen, but you can let it happen by working at it." The same advice holds for colleagues (as in the case of Tim and Harold) or for supervisor and subordinate.

In an effective cowboy-and-horse work team, both the cowboy and the horse need to have as much deep and insightful knowledge of each other in relation to the work at hand as possible. In many work teams, team members need a profound knowledge of those with whom they work; their supervisor needs such a profound knowledge. Work teams vary widely: some work teams are more like swim teams and other work teams are more like SWAT teams. On a swim team, even with outstanding individual performances, the team can compete poorly. In a SWAT team, each team member must know what the other team members are thinking and feeling, as well as knowing their strengths and weaknesses without any communication. If the SWAT team fails, somebody dies. Your work team may not need to function as a SWAT team, but if your team is headed in that direction – maybe the group is acting more like a basketball team or even a baseball team – your team members and team leader need profound and intimate knowledge about each other. For example, in successfully delivering their presentations, Tim and Harold demonstrate profound knowledge of their workshop content, workshop participants, and each other.

Returning to the cowboy-and-horse work team, a cowboy's message is sent to a horse in different ways. When a cowboy looks in a certain direction, the horse will go in that direction. By using muscles and pressure in his legs and rump as he sits on the horse, the cowboy sends signals to the horse; he directs movement, speed, and various other elements critical to working with his horse. Through self-awareness and emotion, the cowboy conveys awareness and emotion to the horse. If the cowboy is calm, his horse will tend to be calm. If the cowboy is anxious, his horse will tend to be anxious.

HORSE SENSE

If the cowboy is calm, his horse will tend to be calm.
If the cowboy is anxious, his horse will tend to be anxious.

Jay Brewer talks about a horse "processing" information. A horse may not be as logical as a human, but it still processes information and makes choices. Jay advises, "Let the horse process and take things in. When the horse is licking his lips, chewing, or yawning, he is processing. Horses can process in the moment, but can't think about the future." So, good leaders and good cowboys recognize when their people and horses are processing information and give them the space required, so everyone can make good choices.

As a supervisor, you can lead anyone to develop a set of roles and responsibilities, creating an environment in which he or she does things mostly right, while having no fear or anxiety. You have to break the work down into smaller, achievable tasks the worker can learn to do effectively. Determining these doable tasks takes patience, insight, and time. In the real world, you may not be able to afford the time and effort to assist or train a worker in this way. In that case, you're responsible for helping the worker find responsibilities that allow him or her to be successful.

As you work with people on developing confidence, optimism, and self-assurance, be careful about paying attention to them as much as to the task. As you define an assignment that expands workers' responsibilities outside their comfort zone, make sure you have the time, resources, and energy to pay attention and be supportive until they carry out the new responsibility correctly. Once they achieve success, you can direct your attention to other places until you have the time and opportunity to continue expanding those workers' responsibilities.

The consistent effort and time you invest up front in this process will require you to focus specifically on how and when you're being attentive to others. This focus takes effort. By taking it on, you'll be deciding to put other issues, and perhaps other people's interests and needs, in the background. However, if you're open, honest, and direct about your decision making and reasoning with everyone involved, each time you refocus on another person you'll start in a good place and make better progress faster. In the long run, you will save time and effort, as long as you commit to the person whose abilities you're developing.

At its core, this chapter focuses on building confidence and trust, thereby keeping fear and anxiety out of the workplace. The first question we posed at the beginning of the chapter was this: How can you keep fear and anxiety away from what people have to do in the workplace? To answer, think about what you do to generate confidence and trust in others. Trust others and they will be inclined to trust you. The best way to build or rebuild trust is through actively engaging in trustworthy acts. Think about what you do to generate fear and anxiety. Perhaps the biggest culprit of those feelings is inconsistency. As W. Edwards Deming states, constancy and consistency of purpose are paramount; inconsistent purpose may be worse than no purpose at all.

Put another way, what can you do to generate trust and security rather than anxiety and fear? The answer is to use strategic planning. Perhaps the most important reason for using strategic planning is that, if conducted correctly, a strategic plan aids in building self-assurance and reduces the likelihood of producing unhealthy anxiety and fear in the workforce.

Consider these few short paragraphs from *Leading People* by Robert Rosen.

> In a complex and chaotic world, a leader who is consistent and predictable helps the people who work for him feel secure. Since they know the ground is not going to shift under their feet, they are open to new ideas. They are willing to take risks.
>
> The converse is also true. If the leader doesn't provide a feeling of security, people find the workaday world a stressful and unpredictable place. People cannot survive under these conditions for too long. They get scared and angry, and unwilling to try much of anything that's new.
>
> A leader can help by providing a feeling of security. Being solid and predictable makes it safe for people to work together, to take risks, and to expose themselves even when the rest of their lives are filled with complexity and chaos.

A leader should address the fear and anxiety in his or her workplace, since these feelings exist in every workplace. The best way to deal with fear and anxiety is to be calm, thoughtful, and consistent.

The second question we posed at the beginning of the chapter was this: How does an environment of fear and anxiety affect people's decisions? A state of fear and anxiety can distract people and sometimes overwhelm them. At any given time, someone's mind may not be clear and he or she may not be at his or her best. Add a little fear and anxiety, and someone may end up making decisions too soon. People may make the wrong decisions or make good decisions about the wrong problems. Overall, fear and anxiety have a big impact on people's decisions because these feelings are not easily put aside; instead, these emotions usually require immediate responses that alleviate them. However, depending on the situation, the impact of a wrong decision isn't always unfavorable.

Some people teach the idea of subjective unit of discomfort (SUD) as a method to achieve peak performance. People are at their best when the SUD is about a 5 on a scale of 1–10. On this scale, 1 indicates sleep and 10 indicates a state of panic. A score of 5, in the middle, indicates an anxiety level equivalent to excitement or being on edge. Harold has found that if he teaches a class or a workshop while he's too relaxed (at, say, an SUD of under 5), he doesn't do a good job. If he's overwhelmed and measuring too far above 5 on the SUD scale, he doesn't do a good job either. Instead, Harold's at his best when he's keyed up, a bit anxious, and on his toes – in other words, at about a 5.

In some instances, a small dose of fear may be appropriate. We've found some people need fear to make a personal change. For example, it's amazing how helpful fear of death can be in coaxing people to change bad health habits. As Samuel Johnson put it, "Depend upon it, sir, when a man knows he is to be hanged in a fortnight, it concentrates his mind wonderfully." Threats of death may not be necessary to obtain a good result in the workplace, of course. In fact, anxiety caused by sheer terror is not helpful. In contrast, anxiety caused by inconsistency and harm is nonproductive. However, anxiety caused by eagerness to do a good job can be productive. Thus, it comes back to you, as the supervisor. In what emotional state do you want your people to learn and perform their work?

CHAPTER 21

WHO ARE YOU?

If you ever teach a horse a lesson in meanness, you'd better hope it doesn't learn the lesson well.

I f you ever teach a horse a lesson in meanness, you'd better hope it doesn't learn the lesson well. In contrast, if you teach people around you kindness, fairness, and generosity, you can hope they do learn those lessons well. People influence the characters of those around them. People also often reap the rewards of what they influence, whether that influence is helpful or harmful.

Have you ever thought to yourself, "Nobody pays attention to what I say or do?" In one sense, this may be true: some people may be so self-absorbed they don't pay attention to what *anyone* else says or does. However, most people do pay attention to who you are. Their attention may be more subconscious than conscious, but they do take notice.

Once, Harold heard a presentation that left a great impression on him. The presenter, a man named Robert, was talking about the day he received his first driver's license. Robert borrowed the family car and drove over to his best friend Jimmy's house so he could take Jimmy for a drive. As Jimmy ran down the porch steps, Jimmy's mother stepped out the front door and called to Robert, "Bobby, remember who you are!"

Jimmy's mother knew Robert had been brought up to be a considerate, conscientious, rule-following person. Because of this, she believed her son was safe as long as Robert remembered who he was. When Harold heard the story, Robert was in his sixties. The experience had remained with him for decades.

So, who are you? This question is different from "What do you do?" or "What are you saying?" This question is a matter of character. Your character is defined by what you think, say, and do when nobody is around. Your character is who you are. Your good character is the primary contributor to productive workplace environments.

Recall the story of Uncle Jim forcing the colt into water. Today Uncle Jim wants to be the kind of person who gives horses the benefit of the doubt. He wants to be the patient and caring individual he once was. Now, despite his past actions with that colt, Uncle Jim understands very well all the things he should have done.

- He should have relaxed on the horse and given the horse time to absorb the rider's confidence.
- He should have demonstrated patience with and taken the time to prepare the horse. He should have encouraged the horse to be comfortable and secure with the change being asked.
- He should have let the horse smell the water.
- He should have watched the horse's body language, then exercised pressure and release (through the reins) to get the colt to test the water with his hoof.

If Uncle Jim had done these things and let the colt take that first step without rushing, the next time they came to a ditch, the horse would have been much more likely just to step into the water. By reviewing his actions with the colt, Uncle Jim realized he needed to be the person he wanted to be and could be again. His experience with Mitchell and the alternator belt also helped Uncle Jim refresh his thinking and adjust his behavior to reveal his true self.

People have unbelievable influence on one another. When others don't seem to pay any attention, don't follow up on what you ask, or don't recognize what you've done, you may feel as if you have little or no influence. The truth is you influence people around you by who you are. Character fairly shouts out to other people. If you are optimistic, faithful, courageous, helpful, caring, and so on, people around you feel safe; they build trust and reflect your helpful traits. However, if you're pessimistic, fearful, disloyal, mean-spirited, uncaring, and so on, people feel insecure; they are unsure of themselves, anxious, and reflect your harmful traits.

Instinctively, humans tend to reciprocate feelings and actions in kind. If people receive kindness, they tend to reciprocate with kindness. If people receive anger, they reciprocate with anger. People teach mostly by example, not as much by what they say (unless the words say the same thing as actions, in which case the words may seem to be an influencing factor), but more by what they do. Actions speak louder than words. Yet, mostly, people influence others through their character.

HORSE SENSE

People have a natural inclination to reciprocate
feelings and actions in kind.

If someone is mean-spirited – of course, no one would want to admit such a thing. However, all people have bad days, or at least bad moments. Have you ever wished ill for someone who slighted you? Have you ever passed on gossip just because it was juicy? Have you ever said, written, or done something anonymously because you didn't want anyone to know it was you? Well, then ...

If people are mean-spirited, they tend to find others who will reciprocate with mean-spiritedness, and together the group builds up an environment of mean-spiritedness. Sooner or later this type of environment will foster mean-spirited action by others outside the group. Those folks will wonder where that action came from. Then, they will most likely reciprocate with more mean-spiritedness. The result is a lesson, taught and received, in how to be mean-spirited.

We prefer a reverse lesson. Think of the topic this way: if you teach kindness, generosity, and support from a place of having a kind and generous disposition (character), you can expect kindness and generosity in return. Meanness is usually not a bottom-up phenomenon. Meanness is a part of company culture that comes from the top down. Evaluate your recent actions: are you teaching kindness or meanness?

As a leader, you're a role model. Some think role modeling relates to skills and process, but role modeling is much more. Role modeling relates to work ethic, attitude, maturity, and more. What people role model is contagious. So, ask yourself what type of role model you, as a leader, supervisor, and manager, want to be in order to bring about the environment you want in your workplace. Compare your role modeling to what you want. If they aren't the same, what do you intend to do to bring the two more into alignment?

As an engineer, whenever the idea of character comes up, Harold asks, "What are the variables [the attributes] of the concept of character?" In *The Power for True Success: How to Build Character in Your Life*, we found a thorough, interesting list of character traits or qualities and included them here, thinking you'd find them interesting too.[5] The qualities are listed as contrasts (or opposites). Even though we don't always see all the pairs as polar opposites, the list is thought-provoking and a bit unnerving.

---

[5] *The Power for True Success: How to Build Character in Your Life* (Institute in Basic Life Principles, Oak Brook, Il., 2001).

CHARACTER QUALITIES

Taken from *The Power for True Success: How to Build Character in Your Life* from the Institute in Basic Life Principles.

Love vs. Selfishness

Alertness vs. Carelessness

Attentiveness vs. Distraction

Availability vs. Self-Centeredness

Boldness vs. Fearliness

Cautiousness vs. Rashness

Compassion vs. Indifference

Contentment vs. Covetousness

Creativity vs. Underachievement

Decisiveness vs. Double-Mindedness

Defference vs. Offensiveness

Dependability vs. Inconsistency

Determination vs. Faintheartedness

Diligence vs. Slothfulness

Discernment vs. Judgment

Discretion vs. Simple-Mindedness

Endurance vs. Discouragement

Enthusiasm vs. Apathy

Faith vs. Unbelief

Flexibility vs. Resistance

Forgiveness vs. Bitterness

Generosity vs. Stinginess

Gentleness vs. Harshness

Gratefulness vs. Murmuring

Honor vs. Disrespect

Hospitality vs. Unfriendliness

Humility vs. Pride

Initiative vs. Idleness

Joyfulness vs. Self-Pity

Justice vs. Fairness

Loyalty vs. Infidelity

Meakness vs. Anger

Obidience vs. Willfulness

Orderliness vs. Confusion

Patience vs. Restlessness

Persuasiveness vs. Contentiousness

Punctuality vs. Tardiness

Resourcefulness vs. Unreliability

Security vs. Anxiety

Self-Control vs. Self-Indulgence

Sensitivity vs. Callousness

Sincerity vs. Hypocrisy

Thouroughness vs. Incompleteness

Thriftiness vs. Extravagance

Tolerance vs. Condemnation

Truthfulness vs. Deception

Virtue vs. Weakness

Wisdom vs. Foolishness

In the end, whether you're working with a horse or with those in the workplace, remember to emphasize the person you are or want to become. While it's important to be other-focused in relationships with other people, you need to be self-focused in your relationship with yourself.

HORSE SENSE

"To understand the horse, you'll find
that you're going to be working on yourself."
– Ray Hunt

Ray Hunt has profound wisdom for us in this regard, writing in *Think Harmony with Horses*:

> To understand the horse, you'll find that you're going to be working on yourself." Ray adds, "I think that a person who doesn't make of himself what he is worthy of is really cheating himself ... We are responsible within ourselves for what happens. Of course you have to get discipline within yourself so that you can have it with your horse. If you don't, this is what will cause your horse to get cranky and take over – [and] get to doing a lot of things wrong.

Before moving on to the next chapter, consider how you might answer the following questions:

- Who are you?
- Who do you want to become so you lead others in the right direction? (Remember, people aren't always sure which qualities make up who they are.)
- Who are you being?
- What are you doing to show who you are and to influence others?

CHAPTER 22

HUMANS ARE FRAGILE

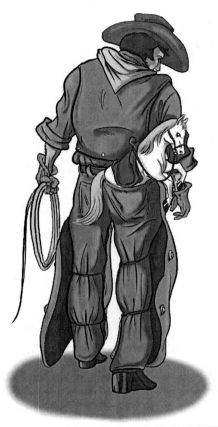

More than anything else, horses want peace.

More than anything else, horses want peace. People may think a horse, or another person, is most interested in what they personally think is important. However, for the most part, horses and people all just want peace. They want to get through each day feeling that they had "a good day." What is a good day?

- A good day means you didn't feel harassed, threatened, incapable, or unworthy.
- A good day lets you finish with a smile of satisfaction and accomplishment.
- A good day encourages you to believe who you are and what you do matters to those people important to you.

A harsher way to state this principle is this: for every second of every minute of every day, the horse is thinking about self-preservation. How does a rider help the horse to put self-preservation aside, in a safe place, so both can focus on the work at hand? As leaders, we need to find ways to add a sense of peace to a horse's, or a subordinate's mind.

The interest of the horse or the person rests on an instinctive foundation of the emotional reactions that have to do with survival. This survival is part of the limbic system (the mammalian brain). People and horses want to survive the day, to know their jobs are safe, and know their lives aren't going to be disrupted by something outside their control. Don't forget people bring threats to their stability and survival from outside the workplace into work. When people feel secure in their days, jobs, and lives, they then can focus on the work you want them to do. As a leader and manager, your job is to find ways a person will feel safe. When people feel safe, they trust. Without trust, you can't lead. Peace can result from trust and the joy of a job well done.

While watching a round-pen demonstration once, horse trainer Lee Caldwell told Tim, "What horses really want, more than anything else, is peace." Lee recalled an experience involving a horse he trained in a round pen. Within the constraints of the sixty-foot circle, the horse stood as far away from the human as possible, keeping a wary eye on Lee's every move. Because the horse hadn't been handled since he was a young colt, he found himself outside his comfort zone. Clearly, Lee had disturbed the horse's peace. As Lee moved toward him, the horse sought even more distance.

First, Lee wanted to train the horse not to turn around and reveal the backside. When a horse shows its backside, the action may indicate whirling to either run or kick, both of which are instinctual for horses when pressured, but unhelpful when forming a partnership. By applying the principle of pressure and release (See the discussion in Chapter 11 about applying small but noticeable pressure and then rewarding any helpful movement by releasing the pressure.), Lee convinced the horse the most peaceful place in the round pen was right next to this formerly scary human. Within ten or fifteen minutes, the basically wild horse went from trying to keep his distance to being in Lee's "back pocket," as he told Tim.

The illustration accompanying this chapter picks up on Lee's comment. Is the cowboy's back pocket a place of control or of peace? Of course, the answer depends on the situation and the cowboy's attitude. When the horse feels a sense of peace, the cowboy gets more cooperation.

What attitudes (in himself or the horses) might a horse trainer have to encourage so the horses lose that sense of peace? Obviously, the answers to this question will be unhelpful. (Consider the outcome of a similar question for supervisors and their direct reports.) Horse trainers aren't angry, domineering, or stubborn when they direct the horse to change direction. The trainers are focused, clear, and consistent; moreover, they take action to remove pressure when appropriate, thus creating a space in which the horse finds the peace it wants. In this scenario, the horse has no need for self-preservation. In contrast, returning to the story at the beginning of Part III, when

Uncle Jim was fragile and too busy with self-preservation, he was unable to connect with others. As a result, he projected a sense of fear and anxiety and did not give the horses he encountered a sense of peace.

Today, an effective leader draws on two differences from the old way, or Theory X approach to supervision, of doing things.

1. According to the old way, leaders made decisions while encouraging fear. However, leaders today find better performance results when they make decisions based on encouraging trust.

2. Using the old way, leaders kept information from those they led because they believed subordinates only needed to know the facts and information pertaining to their specific tasks. Leaders didn't want to overwhelm people with unnecessary, sometimes confusing, extraneous information.

Today, we find, through the presence of abundantly available information and an explosion in advanced technology, leaders can no longer keep people in the dark and expect subordinates' commitment and motivation. Generally speaking, we look back and realize it's unlikely people ever did a poorer job because they had too much information.

Paul Torgersen, past president of Virginia Tech, industrial engineer, and expert in organizational development and management, says: "Humans are fragile." In other words, all people have issues. Many times, because they feel unworthy, people need to develop self-confidence. They're pessimistic or their perception of reality is skewed. Perhaps they never had a boss who mentored them, supported them, or helped them be all they could be. Perhaps they

have dying parents, sick children, friends who are upset with them, or marriages in difficulty. Alternatively, they may have an emotional, mental, or physical illness they don't wish to reveal to anyone else.

Overall, humans approach others with fragility in confidence, attentiveness, or motivation, and sometimes in all three. Often, they're distracted, worrying about how supervisors might translate life's difficulties into poor workplace performance. You may be thinking people with these kinds of problems are few and far between. In our experience, just about every one of us carries worries, hurts, or apprehensions we have to overcome each and every day to concentrate and contribute to the workplace.

Each person poses a threat to these fragile humans who seek peace of mind in the workplace and in life. If you're a boss, you decide who gets what choice or not-so-choice assignment, who gets tasks involving travel and who doesn't, and who gets the raise or promotion and who doesn't. If you're a colleague, you decide how much you'll support and contribute to your work team, along with what your personal priorities are at work. If you're an employee, you decide how much to commit and for how long to your boss and colleagues.

Each of us is fragile and can affect someone else's fragile life. Because of this, people have a huge responsibility to be respectful and considerate of each individual they deal with. When a person is distracted, unresponsive, irritable, confused, reluctant, or distant, first try to see that person as genuinely human, rather than incapable or lazy. Be cordial, attentive, respectful, encouraging, and considerate whenever you encounter someone else.

Many don't realize how significant a genuine and attentive "Good morning" or "How's it going?" is for someone who needs a lift. Often, "How's it going?" is a perfunctory question; people don't expect and don't particularly want a truthful answer. When you give someone else a greeting, it's essential to pause as if you'd like an answer, because you are interested in the answer, and you are interested in the other person. When you get a response, practice your attentive listening skills (remember the SOLAR acronym: square, open, lean forward, appropriate eye contact, relaxed). People don't realize how significant a genuine and attentive courtesy statement such as "Have a good evening" or "Have a great weekend" is when people are leaving the workplace to deal with the rest of their lives.

We believe most people have no idea to what extent their coworkers are concerned with self-preservation. The truth is they are concerned about their job and employment. They are also concerned about the future and their professional development. Finally, they are concerned about life outside work and whether it will be fulfilling.

At work, you might think some people spend a lot of time on the phone or guess they are thinking about playing golf or watching a movie this coming weekend. That's just the surface, though. You don't know what issues are being discussed or what that golf game really entails.

Self-preservation has to do with people's health, employment, family, responsibilities, and relationships. When you interact with someone at work, remember that person consciously or subconsciously needs support, reassurance, a chance to smile or laugh, or the possibility of a hope fulfilled. Each individual has the power to meet these needs or to take away the opportunity to have these needs fulfilled. Whether you give or take away in those instances can make the difference in creating and maintaining a motivated, committed, excited, happy, contributing, and productive workplace, as well as creating and maintaining an environment of community, meaning, and dignity.

Most natural horse trainers view brothers Tom and Bill Dorrance as the people who first began thinking about, practicing, and writing about this new approach to horse training. In *True Unity: Willing Communication between Horse and Human*, Tom's underlying point is that a horse seeks self-preservation first. Tom explains:

> It is their [horses'] natural instinct of self-preservation that the person needs to understand in order to gain the confidence of the horse ... Then, if a person can present himself or herself to the horse in a way that is understandable to the horse, so it can develop confidence, I find the horse is so forgiving ... I'm trying to stress the importance *of the horse*, of really seeing the horse as a horse, of seeing what he is and his potential ... I want to help the person to be able to approach his or her horse with acceptance, assurance, and understanding, to work toward *true unity*. And I try to offer the person the same ... He needs to realize how the person's approach can assure the horse that he can have his self-preservation and still respond to what the person is asking him to do."

HORSE SENSE

"If a person can present himself or herself to the horse in a way that is understandable to the horse, so it can develop confidence, I find the horse is so forgiving."
— Tom Dorrance

Technically speaking, a horse is a prey animal, instinctively on guard against threats from a predator animal. Prey animals tend to bunch up (also known as the herd instinct); they are more skittish and easily startled than predator animals are. Sudden unfamiliar movements trigger their natural fear, which leads to panic, which in turn leads to flight. This division is true of all animals. We end up with flight animals (horses) and fight animals (wolves). In addition, we also have freeze animals (deer caught in the headlights). Different humans can be all these types and/or each of these types at certain times. If you observe people in the workplace, you'll notice these different types by their behavior.

In describing a human's responsibilities when dealing with horses in *Natural Horse*Man*Ship*, Pat Parelli writes:

> Act like a partner, not like a predator. To not act like a predator, the human must be mentally, emotionally, and physically fit. Mental fitness means to learn the natural knowledge about horses; emotional fitness means to be stable to deliver good leadership; and physical fitness means to be able to ride the horse and stay out of his way.

These words are also apt when dealing effectively with people at work. You don't ride people in the same way you would ride a horse; yet, when interacting with them, you do need to be physically present and, at the same time, stay out of their way.

HORSE SENSE

"Act like a partner, not like a predator."

— Pat Parelli

Even when you work hard to build an environment of trust, you'll find fear. There's fear in every organization to a greater or lesser extent. Even in the most trusting workplace, something can come up and generate fear. For a horse, fear is generated by surprises, such as encountering a snake, seeing changing or unsettled weather, or even spying a sudden movement in the surroundings. Likewise, people all confront surprises in the workplace. Your job, as a leader, is to help people in the workplace feel safe knowing surprises are something they can deal with, not worry about. Because fear and trust can't coexist, trust will drive out fear. As we discussed in Chapter 17, your job as a leader is to accurately assess the needs of your people and adequately meet those needs. This way, you show an appropriate type of love in the workplace and fear will leave.

As discussed in Chapter 19, haven't all of us been metaphorically kicked in the face, either in the workplace or in life? Unfortunately, Uncle Jim was metaphorically kicked in the face one too many times, so his open heart didn't last and his natural connection with animals disappeared. While Uncle Jim isn't physically fragile, recovering from an insult to his heart was another story. His injured heart closed. From that moment on, he was living with fear and wasn't open to facing that fear head on. Once he decided to start opening his heart again, he began to heal and move forward.

Ultimately, when you encounter an issue that typically leads to fear, your job is to pause, identify what the issue is, and to face up to the issue. To assess an issue, consider the following questions:

- What's the issue?
- What's frightening?
- What are the steps to deal with this issue?
- What's the first step?
- How do we do the first step?
- How will our strengths help us succeed at this step and at the following steps?

CHAPTER 23

YOU NEED CREATIVE, PRODUCTIVE THINKING

Get your horse to think with you.

G et your horse to think with you. As a rider, you want your horse's mind working with you at all times. While horses don't think in the same way people do, they do act on instinct and training. A cowboy considers his horse to be a thinking partner because the horse acts purposefully, according to the work at hand. When both cowboy and horse approach the work as a team, their partnership is effective. The team can't afford for one of its members to head off in one direction while the other member is working in the opposite direction.

In the workplace, you want your team to work in harmony. What's more, to work in harmony, you want everyone's most creative and productive thinking. As leader, your responsibility is to provide the people you work with the right information, materials, and time so they can be creative and productive. People are thinking creatively when they think of something new and different. They're being productive and innovative when they do something new and different. In the workplace, your team needs to think creatively and then follow through with innovation and productivity.

One of Harold's pronouncements in his organizations is this: "For excellent contributions at work, I want your 'shower time.'" By "shower time" he means those times when people are free to think deeply and imaginatively. We don't know where each person does his or her best and most creative thinking, but, for Harold, it's in the shower. His second-best place for creative thinking is driving an automobile. However, this place is unfortunate because of Harold's need to write down his ideas before he forgets them. Harold's third-best place for creative thinking is on the treadmill (he runs for one hour, three times a week). Significantly, Harold often identifies an issue on which he needs to spend creative time before he gets on the treadmill. This way, he subconsciously sets himself up to be creative. This method works – for him.

It's helpful to be able to be creative and productive under pressure or in unusual situations. For example, think back to the story about Uncle Jim. After their vehicle broke down, Uncle Jim's thinking became creative and productive when he realized his relationship with Mitchell was important enough to change his method

for dealing with the situation. Uncle Jim showed creativity when he repeated things in different ways so Mitchell could understand. The end result was clearly a productive move forward for both Uncle Jim and Mitchell.

When people are forewarned of a need requiring careful consideration and creativity, they tend to store the need in their subconscious minds. Then, when they're asleep or least aware of the need, ideas appear both subconsciously and consciously. Thus, something like shower time is often more valuable than standard nine-to-five business time. In nine-to-five time, people tend to get carried along in routine, repetitive, and noncreative activities. They are interrupted and distracted by people and events throughout the day, and they can't find time to think clearly and completely. Their brains and creative juices are on hold. However, when in the shower, walking in the park, driving, on the treadmill, or wherever an individual goes to have his or her best thinking time, people can dream up contributions to help their organizations be more competitive and more responsive to clients. Thinking is work. Every writer will tell you that typing is the easy part of being a writer. It's knowing what to type that matters.

Taking a larger view, a good leader should nurture his or her people's shower time, so they can be prepared to creatively and productively contribute in meetings and other important business activities. This free, unstructured time is one reason why outside problems, such as a sick family member or a difficult relationship, can have a harmful effect on the workplace. If one of your people has a personal problem, guess what's on his or her conscious and subconscious mind during free time? If your employee is consumed with family, health, or relationship problems at work, chances are he or she will spend down time on those worries, rather than on being creative and productive in his/her work. Yet you want your employees' conscious minds to be generating ideas for your company. So, you need to be cognizant of the demands you place on people in the workplace and know people have demands outside the office affecting their health and their relationships. As a leader, consider more than just the daily activities at work when you evaluate the people you lead. You want their minds working with you not only during work, but also at those times when their minds are at their best.

These ideas apply on horseback too. As Louis Wood explains, "If a horse doesn't know how to deal with the situation, the horse will flee the situation mentally." You don't want to lose the horse's attention. Without focusing on the job at hand, a horse (with its herd mentality) is going to consider getting back to the other horses. Then, the horse won't be tuned into its work.

One way to prevent this and get the horse to think with you is to give it freedom to be "thoughtful." Since horses don't have the same brains as humans do, being thoughtful in horse terms means not being distracted or disturbed. So, don't distract the horse or disturb its routine as it goes about its work. You want the horse to have the freedom to be alert and aware of the work and of what you're doing. You can determine the horse's alertness through its body language. For example, if a horse is alert, its ears perk up and its gait is sprightlier.

Similarly, in the workplace, a distracted person rarely seems focused. This situation in which the horse loses attention and shifts its focus to other horses can be seen in the office too. Once a person loses focus on the task at hand, the nearby extroverts will start considering interacting with others in the office. The nearby introverts will fall silent and withdraw.

HORSE SENSE

*You can determine the horse's alertness through
its body language. For example, if a horse is alert,
its ears perk up and its gait is sprightlier.*

As supervisor, you want your work team to have a flow and you want team members to go with that flow. This work typically flows through a process. (We discuss the importance of process in Chapter 14.) However, there's a comfortable flow of relationship when people work well together. People are able to read each other and are considerate of one another. They're not just being polite when they're considerate; they are other-focused, considering the other people as they do their work.

In workshops we encourage people to participate in an exercise about competition, cooperation, and collaboration. This exercise is a physical game in which people have to accomplish a task together. In part of the exercise one person works at the task, which is employing a physical apparatus. When the time comes to hand the apparatus off to the next team member, the first person usually doesn't consider the following person's preferences, as described in the following questions:

- Does the next person prefer the apparatus to be facing in the same orientation you prefer?
- People tend to pass the apparatus according to their preferred orientation.

- For example, is one person right-handed and the other left-handed?
- Is the second person comfortable with the speed and firmness with which the first person hands off the apparatus?
- Is what the first person did with or to the apparatus clear to the second person?
- Does the first person need to provide some information along with the apparatus? If so, what information?
- Was the first person aware and considerate of the second person in terms of what he or she needs and must deal with?

In the workshop exercise, when it's time to hand off the apparatus, the receiver is tuned into the handoff and eager to perform well. When the first worker is distracting or disruptive, the next worker loses focus and may not instantly know how to deal with the apparatus's unexpected and uncomfortable orientation, with the speed and firmness of the handoff, or with the lack or kind of information provided by the first worker. At that point, the second worker becomes unsure about how to deal with the orientation, speed, firmness, or information the first worker has provided.

At this point, the second worker is dealing with emotions such as frustration, confusion, and even anger or fear. He or she is no longer tuned into the work but rather, tuned into feelings that distract from best efforts.

Ask yourself the following:

- Which attitude yields the best team performance?
- Is it more helpful if team members adapt to how I prefer to do things?

- Is it more helpful if I learn how to help team members make their contribution to the task better?

In the workshop exercise, after each individual discusses how team members prefer to deal with the apparatus, the answer is clear. People need to be other-focused in their interactions with each individual team member.

Distraction happens in the workplace all the time; people are consumed by daily duties, interruptions, and surprises. People have to react to those daily interferences, which often seem to consume a disproportionately large amount of time and consideration. Therefore, nobody should be surprised our creative, productive thinking occurs outside the office. Consider a situation in which someone is walking alone on the beach, has a good idea, and runs to a phone to tell a team member about that idea. This person wasn't trying to have an idea about a particular work issue but just walking on the beach. Yet, because this person was relaxed and not overwhelmed by the distractions of work details, he or she was free to be thoughtful.

Some people can be more creative when they encounter a problem or idea that has become apparent, either by being described by someone else or generated by their own interest. They may need time to internalize the problem or idea and figure out how to best solve it, using either what they know or their specific talents or skills. They need time and creative thinking to relate to past experiences, all of which they can then apply to the current problem. People can be creative when they apply their uniqueness to situations. Then, they will own the results.

Where is your best place for creative thinking? Protect that space and prepare yourself to be creative. Try to develop and protect this type of place for your people as well; encourage them to think creatively.

CHAPTER 24

BE AWARE OF YOUR ATTITUDE'S INFLUENCE

Your horse will emulate your attitude,
so choose your attitude thoughtfully.

Your horse will emulate your attitude, so choose your attitude thoughtfully. Your attitude is your disposition or feeling about your work, your workplace, a relationship, or your horse. You view work and others through the lens of your attitude. In short, your attitude affects how you deal with the world.

We believe the concepts of *love* and *hate* are more about attitude and personal choice, rather than the feelings most people think they are. A significant part of love is the attitude of caring. Conversely, a significant part of the opposite of love is not caring. We believe not caring is, essentially, an attitude of indifference. Love and hate, caring and indifference, trust and distrust, attentive and disinterest, are all choices. Since you choose your attitude, choose your attitude carefully.

People allow themselves to become angry depending on the situation or the person they're dealing with. Have you ever noticed how you allow yourself to become angry when one person says or does something, yet, when another person does or says the same thing, you don't get angry? Alternatively, perhaps you don't become angry when a person you love does something one time, yet the next time, you find yourself reacting with anger to the same person doing the same thing. So, maybe you shouldn't blame a person for *making* you angry. You're actually choosing anger. You may not think you have a choice, but you do.

Let's return to the story of Uncle Jim. After he closed his heart, he found he just couldn't hide his hurt, frustration, distrust, or anger. Horses sensed his emotions and were frightened away. (With their instinct for self-preservation, horses always leave room enough to flee a potential danger.) While Uncle Jim realized a slow transformation was occurring, he was emotionally stuck. He didn't know how to move on and reacquire the open heart he'd possessed during his glory days.

Natural horse trainer Jay Brewer explains when a cowboy asks a horse to come to him and then turns his back on the horse, the horse will think the cowboy doesn't care about him. Sending the message that you don't care can destroy an effort to build a relationship with either a horse or a person. As Jay says, when a horse turns his back on the cowboy, the horse doesn't want to see the cowboy. The horse is hoping the cowboy (and the potential work) will just go away. Instead, when Jay is ready to work, he wants the horse's eyes and ears on him; he wants the horse's attention. He wants mutual caring about the partnership and the work. How many times does a mother say to her child, "Look at me when I talk to you"? When a mother sees her child look into her eyes, she believes her message has a better chance of being accepted.

As a leader, you want to maintain and project an attitude of caring and attentiveness. By showing supervisees how much you care about your work, you influence others to care and encourage them to do their very best. In Chapter 17 we discussed the appropriate expression of love in the workplace and how the workplace version differs from the appropriate expression of love in the family unit. When you use these expressions of love, you're caring for another person. In this chapter, we discuss caring about your work or your relationships. Caring is somewhat different from love. When you care about something, you show deep interest and concern.

Here are five rules you should care about:

- To care about your work is to be committed and involved. Caring leads to you and others buying in to the work team's mission, vision, and principles.
- When you care enough, you hold yourself accountable.
- To care is to be part of something bigger than yourself, which leads to partnership.
- When you care about the work and the work team, you enjoy your work and your relationships. You find joy.
- To care is to be open to learning.

When a horse cares, it will not show indifference. Instead, the horse will go the extra mile and extend itself. To get more from a horse, help it care.

When you care, others return your caring attitude. You set up a reciprocating cycle focused on the growth of caring, attentiveness, inquisitiveness, interest, and concern.

HORSE SENSE

When a horse cares, it will not show indifference. Instead, the horse will go the extra mile and extend itself. To get more from a horse, help it care.

Early in his life, Uncle Jim had an open heart: he cared about teaching and learning about animals, and he had a patient and attentive attitude. His attitude affected the people and animals around him. These people and animals reciprocated his attitude, and Uncle Jim's caring for those around him increased.

Remember, in your interactions with others, you get to choose between love, hate, caring, and indifference. *Indifference* means not to care or to be dispassionate (no love, no hate), as demonstrated by a lack of interest or concern. By saying, "I don't care," you show indifference. The minute you say, "I don't care about [this thing or person]," you're sending strong signals of indifference:

- "I don't care about that client."
- "I don't care what tasks you give me to do."
- "I don't care when we meet on that issue."

Of course, usually you do care, and very deeply. However, when you make these statements, you're communicating and teaching indifference.

Indifference is poison to the spirit. Being indifferent shuts everything and everyone down. Teaching indifference guides others into a stale, bland, and sad state of existence. To avoid this, you need to ask yourself whether you could be more empathetic more often.

The most unfeeling (lack of feeling) and harmful approach you can have toward your relationship with another person or toward your work is indifference, because when you're indifferent you're conveying the impression that a person or your work doesn't matter to you. Indifference can be a contagious disease. People in an organization can easily pass indifference around among their groups.

A cowboy and a horse can pass the disease of indifference between themselves, which is what happened with Uncle Jim and the colts. Because of his hardships, he chose to live with an attitude of indifference. Horses and other animals, as well as the people around him, responded in kind, and the indifferent cycle continued. Later in life, Uncle Jim became eager to reverse this cycle. For him, the best way to reverse the cycle was to identify something or someone he cared about (for example, his nephew, Mitchell) and focus on that. This approach to reversing the cycle is similar to the approach we use for developing and fostering exceptional moments, as discussed in Chapter 18.

People can show indifference in many ways. They can show indifference by behavior: shrugging off the idea, the activity, or the person. Alternatively, people can use words that carry an indifferent tone of voice or are accompanied by indifferent body language. Learn to spot indifference in others and in yourself. After you learn to see indifference in yourself or in your behaviors, you can work on getting out of an indifferent or disinterested frame of mind by using behaviors that reveal attention and interest. Usually, indifference isn't helpful, unless that indifference helps you protect yourself in coping with a potentially painful situation.

The cowboy in the illustration that accompanies this chapter is demonstrating an unhelpful attitude: perhaps it is indifference, stubbornness, or some other attitude we don't want the horse to emulate. The horse may be confused by this attitude or, most likely, may be paying rapt attention to the attitude, preparing to emulate it.

Parents with teenagers know very well a popular, indifferent response that can be used to answer a variety of questions: "I don't care." (Some people carry the attitude of this response into the workplace too.) How many parents have had the following conversation?

"Would you prefer steak or chicken for dinner?"

"I don't care."

"Would you like to go to the movies or play golf?"

"I don't care."

This answer conveys an indifference that goes beyond simple neutrality. It's an indifference that causes a back to be turned, a hope to be defeated, and an idea to die. We hope this teenager means, "I like both steak and chicken, and I'm having difficulty choosing." Alternatively, perhaps the teenager means, "What goes into my body doesn't matter because I'm hungry and any food will meet my need." Difficult decisions are a healthy part of life. Perhaps this phrase carries a less positive meaning, such as, "You don't matter to me." Beware even the perception of indifference.

By caring, you position yourself to be other-focused, so you recognize a person's strengths and can affirm, encourage, and gather those strengths to move them toward a common vision. When it's

clear someone cares about you, who you are, what you contribute, what you contend with, or what you need, that person is communicating you matter to him or her. *Each person has a fundamental need to matter.* We believe there's no greater empowering idea than believing you matter. Furthermore, when you care about others in this way, whether at home or at work, you're telling them they matter to you personally. Communicating the idea that others matter and you care shows the opposite of indifference.

People act out caring in the workplace by learning about other people and their work. If people care, they want to learn about others: where they come from, what brings joy and hope, and what's difficult. People also want to learn about the work: what the contribution is, what's needed, and what gets in the way.

Overall, people have a need to communicate caring and being cared for, or at least respected. So, how do you live out your caring about your work and your workplace relationships?

- By practicing all the communication skills related to active listening
- By actively listening and thus sending the message you're open to influence
- By being open to influence

Demonstrate others matter by changing the way you might normally do things to accommodate their thoughts, needs, or wants. Then, those people know they matter to you. When people use oral communication, they verify their openness to influence by reflecting the emotion and content of the message being sent. By truly being curious (as in wonderment, not as in interrogation) about another person's well-being, responsibilities, problems, and needs, you send the message that you care.

The partnership between horse and cowboy is all about learning: learning about each other in building a relationship, learning about the task at hand, and learning the strengths and skills each of the partners must bring to the work. In this type of relationship and in workplace relationships, we believe learning and loving are the keys to living well.

Remember, you get what you expect. Expectation includes the Pygmalion effect, in which you live up to the expectations others have of you, and the Galatea effect, in which you live up to the expectations you have of yourself. So, if you expect indifference, you'll get indifference, not only from yourself but also from those around you. (We discuss the Pygmalion and Galatea effects in Chapter 7.)

Let's return to the story of Uncle Jim one more time. After experiencing heartbreak, Uncle Jim became demanding of people and horses, which was especially evident in his unreasonable expectations. He started to expect people and horses to learn immediately and just know how to do what he expected of them, even though he subconsciously knew that, to learn, humans and horses need support (through patience and repetition). While he never abused people or horses (because he knew better), Uncle Jim became irrationally short-tempered; he shut down and became unapproachable. Both people and horses recognized his impatient and irritable body language and tone of voice. In other words, he stopped being able to lead.

Today's approach to leadership includes the basic premise that we (the leaders) are not here to be served, but to serve others. However, leaders shouldn't think their needs can't be met at the same time as others' needs; instead, leaders simply have to rethink what their needs are. If these needs are so different from the needs that can be met in any given situation, maybe the leaders are doing the wrong things. If people can't be happy serving others in a certain capacity because serving others makes them feel unimportant or unworthy, then they're not doing the right jobs. Leaders are here to serve clients, bosses, peers, and subordinates. They work to contribute talents, ideas, efforts, and their best. In sum, practicing servant leadership shows a leader cares.

When leaders have effective relationships with clients, they serve those clients by giving best efforts and results; in turn, the clients serve the leaders by giving them challenging work and a livelihood. Leaders serve their bosses by being responsive and dedicated, while their bosses serve by giving guidance and support. Leaders serve their peers by giving them assistance and attention; peers serve them by returning the favor. Finally, leaders serve subordinates by giving them guidance and support; the subordinates serve by being responsive and dedicated.

One concept we've learned over the years is each person wants others to understand and care about his or her job and responsibilities. If a person trusts you, he or she would love to teach you about the ins and outs of the work and who he or she is.

When one of his grandchildren responds to a question about steak or chicken with, "It doesn't matter," Harold's concern is how big the emotional leap is from "It doesn't matter" to "I don't matter." "It doesn't matter" is a form of indifference. "It doesn't matter" is similar to "I don't care." Remember, you can teach indifference in small and subtle ways. You model indifference by not caring or by carelessly using language that communicates not caring. Indifference is an attitude that can be picked up by a horse or a person. As a leader, you need to make sure you don't harbor that kind of attitude, and you need to be attentive to that attitude in others. You can confront that attitude in others in caring ways. "Of course you matter!" certainly isn't threatening. Be mindful, though, that confrontations such as this carry an impact.

Ultimately, don't role model and teach indifference; role model and teach caring instead. Repeatedly and clearly show your expectations for caring attitudes and behavior. People will tend to live up to your expectations, so make sure you model the expectations you really want.

FINAL THOUGHTS

WE MUST MAKE A PLACE

You know you've taught your horse successfully when it demonstrates what it's learned.

You know you've taught your horse successfully when it demonstrates what it's learned. The idea of the relative significance of teaching and learning in horse training originally came from Monty Roberts' video *Sign Up*. The video shows Monty Roberts using natural horse training techniques to "break" a horse. As mentioned earlier in this book, Roberts prefers to "start" a horse, not "break" a horse. In *The Man Who Listens to Horses*, he writes, "I had come to think of my process as entirely different from that of 'breaking' horses. That word has connotations of violence and domination … I [call] my method 'starting' horses. If traditional breaking was designed to generate fear in the horse, I wanted to create trust."

The important thing to consider when teaching your horse or your direct reports is this: teaching is linear, while learning is circular. In school, learning is best exemplified in sports and theater. In sports and theater, people receive instruction, practice what they've heard or seen demonstrated, get feedback on how they did, practice again based on the feedback, and get more feedback. This cycle continues until the people get it right. This kind of learning is circular. The best learning comes from mentoring or coaching, not necessarily from teaching. An effective teacher helps a person or horse learn. Did the teacher you remember most coach you or teach you around your homework? After getting your grade on the homework, did you move on to the next lesson without practicing the preceding lesson until you truly learned it? This process is about learning, not teaching. In learning, you're able to extend the lesson beyond the example upon which you originally learned the lesson.

Using the natural horse training approach discussed in his book, Roberts can accomplish what would often take weeks to do in less than an hour. In another book, *Horse Sense for People*, Roberts shares his wisdom about horses in ways that can affect people's relationships at home and at work. He gives advice on everything from communication, trust, and respect to sample blackboards used to encourage good behavior in children.

From the perspective of the cowboy and horse, we might assume the cowboy is the teacher and the horse is the learner. However, the opposite is just as true. The cowboy must learn about the horse and how the animal addresses its work. The horse has its own strengths and fears, and responds best to particular actions or words.

As mentioned in Chapter 3, when we emphasized the importance of listening, Ray Hunt reminds us in *Cowboy Logic* of a very important principle: "The horse will teach you if you'll listen." A horse can't formally teach these things, since it doesn't speak with words; instead, a rider must learn from the horse by having an open mind and carefully observing the horse. In this chapter, we emphasize the importance of teaching and especially learning.

HORSE SENSE

From the perspective of the cowboy and horse,
we might assume the cowboy is the teacher and the horse
is the learner. However, the opposite is just as true.

The importance of learning is also true about the people for whom leaders are responsible. Leaders need to learn the strengths, workflow, needs, difficulties, and parts of work most satisfying to their people. Usually, leaders can't fit workers perfectly into a job assignment in which their every need or interest is met. However, a good leader can show caring by learning about their people and matching the tasks in some way to their interests or strengths. Then, workers have reason to believe the leader is doing his or her best to establish the best fit for the work team and for its members as individuals. A good practice is for leaders to ask their people to "teach" them about their work. In truth, in that scenario, leaders put themselves into a learning mode.

In the workplace, leaders identify what needs to be done. Then, they do their best to get it done. Certainly, when people begin a new task or skill, their best is far from perfect and may be some distance from adequate. At this time, learning can take place. In the end, people must assess what they did and the results of what they did. Then, they determine what they need to do and want to do to improve. They try again. By repeatedly looping through the circular process of getting information about the work, using this information to determine a better way, trying the better way, and assessing the results to get yet more information, people learn. Teaching is providing the information. Yet teaching is often static. Coaching helps people use their own strengths, resources, and experiences to incorporate the new information into their approaches to their own issues and objectives. Learning requires more than teaching or even coaching.

There's more to the learning process and supervision than learning about the person and his or her work. A good leader needs to develop a workplace *culture* conducive to learning. A learning culture provides an environment in which the entire work team is open and honest, learning from one another. Everyone can learn about the work and the interactions of the team members as they perform the work together.

The concept of culture is what we believe in, what we stand for, and "how we do things around here." Culture provides the foundation and the glue to keep the work team going, serving everyone when things get dicey. How is that culture fostered? Jay Brewer says people must *make* a place for learning. People can't really teach, empower, or hold others accountable because those are active verbs that require others to learn, to be empowered, or to be accountable. As leaders and supervisors, what people can do is create places where others can learn, empower themselves, and care enough to hold themselves accountable.

Monty Roberts confirms the need for a culture or environment of learning by saying, "If you're a teacher, you have to create an environment [in which] your student can learn." All supervisors and leaders are teachers at some level when they make places where their people can learn. Of course, no supervisor or leader can make a person learn. Those leaders can only make places where people want to learn. Consider the old saying, "You can lead a horse to water, but you can't make him drink." You can provide a learning opportunity, but you can't force a person to learn.

So, you can't make a person learn. You can make a place where he or she finds it safe and invigorating to learn. You can offer workers such a place and support them in learning by offering encouragements and affirmations, while providing methods and resources to use what they learn. That's it. The workers will take advantage of the place and learn, or they won't.

Monty Roberts adds, "You can't take knowledge and push it into a brain. The brain has to pull it in." You can put the knowledge out there and make it available. You can send the message. However, there's more work to do. You have to make a place where a person *wants* what you've made available. You push information out of one brain so another brain can pull it in. Unfortunately, it won't work the other way around.

Finally, you need to make sure you push out information that's worth being pulled in. You need to provide timely, accurate, and relevant information. So, instead of focusing on causing people to learn (which you can't do; that's more like teaching), you can provide good information, the place in which to learn, and support to help a worker use that information during a learning process.

Learning takes time. People need time to go through all the steps in the circular learning process. Moreover, they need time to loop through the steps of the learning process as many rounds as necessary to ensure learning happens. Looping or spiraling is intended to take people (and horses) to higher and higher levels of understanding. Louis Wood describes the need for a place in which learners can experience the spiraling: "We need to build a foundation of learning for the horse to build on to higher and higher levels." You won't get that time and looping without a learning environment. The leader is responsible for making such a place in any workplace.

The most daunting part of real learning is people never reach the end. We can all always learn more. Most obviously and abruptly, we fail to learn our way to perfection when we quit the learning process. One definition of success and failure is as long as we continue to learn, we'll work our way to success. When we quit learning, we fail. Real learning takes motivation, persistence, and, in many situations, courage. We believe humans' reasons for being are to learn and to love. In truth, these two activities aren't very different.

The place a leader makes in the workplace forms a foundation to support the continual learning people need to reach the maturity they seek through their learning. In *Cowboy Logic*, Ray Hunt admonishes, "Believe in your horse so your horse can believe in you." How would this logic relate to workers? Consider this: if you don't believe in your people, how can they believe in you?

"Horses teach riders and riders teach horses," Pat Parelli says in *Natural Horse*Man*Ship*. Notice the circularity in this statement: horse and rider mature in their understanding of their task and of each other. Pat continues, "This is such an important principle.

Many good horsemen say that horses are their best teachers. There's a reason for this. For example, if you want to learn how to cut cattle [from a herd], buy a trained cutting horse to learn from. He'll teach you about the sport and what it feels like to cut a cow so you can understand it better." Do you think coworkers who have been doing a task for a while can teach you a lot about what's involved in doing the task? Perhaps they can share some tricks of the trade. They will tell you much about the task if they trust you. So, that's what you want to do when you make a place where everyone can teach and everyone can learn.

Just like the cowboy who's regularly working with his horse, if a partnership is dealing with any kind of challenges, you'll encounter difficulties in that relationship as you work with people. The question usually isn't whether a relationship will be strained by the difficulty, because the relationship most likely will be. Instead, the question is whether the relationship will come out of the difficulty stronger. If so, you're developing an enduring relationship through your efforts. And what is an enduring relationship? On the face of it, one might say an enduring relationship is a long-lasting relationship. We think there's more. An enduring relationship endures difficulties and comes out stronger. People encounter a similar situation in physical fitness. Individuals stress their muscles with weights to break them down: a healthy body will not only recover from the strain, but will build stronger muscles.

How can you help a relationship come through a difficulty and be stronger on the other side?

- First, build trust by committing trustworthy acts (which are as simple as being on time to a meeting) and build respect (which you can foster by asking yourself about the other person's strengths and why you appreciate them).

- Second, recognize a challenging task or situation for what it is; then, identify the helpful or enjoyable aspects of that task or situation.
- Third, identify how you and the other person can collaborate and create something together when dealing with the task or situation.
- Fourth, affirm and reinforce what each of you brings to the resolution of the task or situation.

An enduring relationship will not only recover from the difficulty, but will become stronger and deeper.

Enduring relationships nourish life. They develop between people who understand themselves at a deep level, are emotionally mature, and are personally strong in character. People in enduring relationships aren't emotionally enmeshed; they maintain their own identities and appreciate their partners for their strengths.

In and out of enduring relationships, there's a big difference between what you can and can't do to manage, lead, and supervise effectively. Here are the actions or ideas we believe you can't cause a person to do or think:

1. You can't make a person learn.
2. You can't empower a person.
3. You can't hold a person accountable.
4. You can't force a person to trust or respect you.
5. You can't compel a person to seek help, even when he or she would benefit from help.
6. You can't make your people appreciate others' strengths.

7. You can't cause a person to stop selfish behavior.

8. You can't require your people to meet unclear, unspoken, or misunderstood expectations.

9. You can't hand someone the attitude of joy.

10. You can't dictate love.

If you can't do these things, what can you do?

We believe you can make a place where all of the following can be achieved:

1. Each person hungers to learn and grow to his or her full potential.

2. Each person is encouraged to feel empowered by developing confidence, optimism, trust, self-esteem, purpose, and loyalty.

3. Each person cares enough to hold him- or herself accountable;

4. trust and respect grow through the joys and difficulties of building enduring relationships.

5. People are comfortable seeking help when and as needed;

6. strengths are sought, discovered, affirmed, encouraged, and appreciated.

7. Being other-focused is the norm.

8. Expectations are clear and understood.

9. The organization's emerging property is joy.

10. With readiness and willingness, people accurately assess and adequately supply other people's needs.

To be truly successful, you must make such a place.

SUMMARY

People *lead* through *strengths*.

Ultimately, a leader surrenders to others' strengths. Listening, and especially reflection, puts you in the leadership and the power position. Reflection is how you learn about others' strengths. Leaders have great focus and they train that focus on a shared vision. Leaders enhance others' strengths through encouragement.

People *supervise* by setting and meeting *expectations*.

Setting expectations begins the management (decision making) process, while meeting expectations reinforces that process's success. Supervisees want clarity, especially of expectations. Good supervisors help facilitate change, all while thinking steps ahead in moving toward process closure. In turn, supervisors understand unintended consequences and the importance of pressure and release.

People *manage* well if they recognize
the value of *relationships* with others.

People show love in the workplace when they decide to learn about and meet others' needs. People improve relationships and work through learning and internalizing their exceptional moments. Leaders manage and supervise for the best among groups. Leaders manage best when they know themselves, others, and their impact on others.

People can make places where *strengths* are encouraged, *expectations* are clear, and *relationships* endure.

Leaders can make such places by focusing on loving, learning, and being other-focused. The value of a management process is that it enables leaders to streamline what they understand well about the work so they make room (in time and effort) for the team's creativity in better serving the client and coworkers.

Note: The principles discussed in this book relate to natural horse training and the Theory Y approach to supervision. For those who cling to old-school training or the Theory X supervision approach, the ideas in this book will be foreign and maybe even ludicrous. We hope, as you've been reading through the various chapters, you've found these new-world approaches appealing and useful. We believe workers' mindsets have changed over the years. Today workers expect to be treated fairly, are willing to take responsibility, and want to contribute and be productive. They want to make a difference.

PART III

RELATIONSHIPS AT A GLANCE

CHAPTER 17:
YOU CAN'T HIDE THE CONDITION
OF YOUR HEART

1. Horses and people: if you try to lead them without loving them, you'll fail them.

2. First, let's define *love* in the workplace: to love is to accurately assess and adequately meet another person's need. For love among family members, we'll adjust the definition by changing two words: to love is to accurately assess and abundantly satisfy another person's need.

3. Being valued, appreciated, respected, understood, and safe helps establish a place in which people can best empower themselves and display their unique strengths and resources.

4. According to systems theory, a group of people who spend time together will develop an emotional system. The bottom line is, people can't help but be influenced by the moods, attitudes, and emotions of those closest to them. Remember, the passing of emotion is instinc-

tive. Just as horses pass agitation when they're feeling it, people pass agitation in the workplace.

5. You can observe how each person influences the group by observing body language and facial expressions and listening to voice tone.

6. People are contagious. Our emotions spread through a group like an epidemic. The good news is you get to choose whether you contribute to an epidemic of comfort and excitement, an epidemic of boredom and disinterest, or an epidemic of panic and agitation.

7. Managers and supervisors need to assess, evaluate, understand, and manage themselves. This practice is called personal mastery. The more of it you have, the better you are as a leader and manager.

CHAPTER 18:
WE CHANGE THROUGH OUR
EXCEPTIONAL MOMENTS

8. Success can be a matter of focus and, ultimately, a matter of exceptional moments.

9. An exceptional moment doesn't have to be a time when the person excelled at the task. The exceptional moment could have been when the person did the task better than usual.

10. Helping those not otherwise inclined to look at the half-full-glass scenario changes their focus; this is how a leader begins to support

the people he or she works with to think favorably about their performance and abilities, thus motivating them to do better.

11. Don't focus on what others do wrong. After doing so, sooner or later, others will quit their relationships with you, either physically or emotionally.

12. Don't focus on what isn't helpful. Address those things, but don't focus on them, because you get what you focus on.

13. A good leader helps people become successful in their own ways by helping them reflect on what they do right and what they bring to the table when they do well.

CHAPTER 19:
THERE'S A GOOD PERSON IN THERE!

14. When people speak, act, or decide, they do so based on their thoughts and feelings. People's feelings give energy to their thoughts so that they act, speak, or decide.

15. We've found each person just wants to get through the day as best he or she can.

16. Once you believe there's good in a person and the person wants to exhibit goodness, it will be almost natural for you to build effective relationships with those who work for you.

17. Haven't all of us been metaphorically kicked in the face, either in the workplace or in life?

18. Because most people are just trying to protect themselves, there's no value or productivity in blaming or retaliating.

19. People should manage themselves and their work based on the best within and among their teams.

CHAPTER 20:
HELPFUL FEELINGS CONTRIBUTE
TO PRODUCTIVE WORKPLACES AND
HARMONIOUS RELATIONSHIPS

20. Think harmony, whether you're working with horses or with subordinates. Life is much more enjoyable with harmony.

21. A harmonious relationship helps people make seamless contributions in which they help each other make efforts and ideas, leading to the group exceeding expectations.

22. Good leaders and good cowboys recognize when their people or horses are processing information. Then, they provide needed space in which their people and horses can work out what is needed. As a result, everyone can make good choices.

23. As you work with people on developing their confidence, optimism, and self-assurance, you must be careful about when you pay attention to those people. Undoubtedly, at some point, you'll

have to reduce or stop your attentiveness, and knowing when and how to reduce or stop paying attention without disrupting the progress you've made together can be difficult. However, if you're successful, when you refocus your attention on those people again, you'll start in a good place and make better progress more quickly. In the long run, you save time and effort by spending time helping your people develop themselves, as long as you commit to each person you're developing.

24. Perhaps the biggest culprit in creating anxiety and fear is inconsistency.

25. The most important reason for strategic planning may be that if it's done right, a strategic plan aids in building self-assurance and reduces the likelihood of producing unhealthy anxiety and fear in the workforce.

26. A leader should address the fear and anxiety that exists in every workplace. The best way to dispel fear and anxiety is to be calm, thoughtful, and consistent.

27. In essence, anxiety caused by inconsistency and harm is non-productive. Anxiety caused by eagerness to do a good job can be productive.

CHAPTER 21:
WHO ARE YOU?

28. If you teach people around you kindness, fairness, and generosity, you can hope they learn the lesson well. You influence the characters of those around you. What's more, you often reap the rewards of what you influence.

29. Character is what people think, say, and do when nobody else is around. Your character is who you are. A leader's good character is the primary contributor to productive workplace environments.

30. Instinctively, humans tend to reciprocate in kind. If people receive kindness, they tend to reciprocate with kindness. If they receive anger, they reciprocate with anger. People teach mostly by example: not as much by what they say (unless the words say the same thing as actions, in which case the words may seem to be an influencing factor), but more by what they do. Actions speak louder than words. Yet, mostly, people influence others through their character.

31. While leaders need to be other-focused in their relationships, they also need to be self-focused and develop a good relationship with themselves.

CHAPTER 22:
HUMANS ARE FRAGILE

32. People want to survive the day, to know their jobs are safe, and know their lives aren't going to be disrupted by something outside

their control. Don't forget people bring threats to their stability and survival from outside the workplace into work. When people feel secure in their days, jobs, and lives, they then can focus on the work you want them to do.

33. As a leader and manager, your job is to find ways a person, or a horse, will feel safe. When people feel safe, they trust. Without trust, you can't lead.

34. A leader is focused, clear, and consistent, yet he or she takes action to remove pressure when appropriate, thus creating an environment in which people find the peace they all want.

35. Humans approach others with fragility in confidence, attentiveness, or motivation, sometimes in all three. Given the fragility of humans, people have huge responsibilities to be respectful to and considerate of each person they deal with. When a person is distracted, unresponsive, irritable, confused, reluctant, or distant, you first need to see that person as genuinely human, rather than as incapable or lazy. Be cordial, attentive, respectful, encouraging, and considerate whenever you come into contact with another person.

36. We believe most people have no idea how much the person who works next to them is concerned with self-preservation.

37. There's fear in every organization to a greater or lesser extent. As a cowboy or as a leader and manager, your job is to help the horse or your people feel safe knowing surprises are something you can deal with, not worry about.

CHAPTER 23:
YOU NEED CREATIVE,
PRODUCTIVE THINKING

38. In the workplace, you want the team to work in harmony; to work in harmony, you need everyone's most creative and productive thinking. As leader, your responsibility is to give the people with whom you work the right information and enough time to be creative and productive.

39. Leaders need people's creativity and intuition more than the perfunctory activities of a typical workday. Whenever and wherever creativity and productivity happen, a good leader wants those who work for him or her to feel free to contribute to the work. If subordinates are consumed with family, health, or relationship problems at work, they'll spend their shower time (unstructured free time) on their worries, not on being creative and productive.

40. Don't distract or disturb the routine of your people while they're going about their work, as long as their effort results in the effective accomplishment of their work.

41. You want your work team to have a good flow, and you want team members to go with the flow.

CHAPTER 24:
BE AWARE OF YOUR
ATTITUDE'S INFLUENCE!

42. Indifference is poison to the spirit. Being indifferent shuts everything and everyone down. Teaching indifference guides others into a stale, bland, and sad state of existence.

43. You can show indifference by your behavior, such as shrugging off an idea, activity, or person. Alternatively, you can use words that carry an indifferent tone of voice or are accompanied by indifferent body language. Learn to spot indifference in others and in yourself. When you learn to see indifference in yourself or your behaviors, you need to work on getting out of an indifferent or disinterested frame of mind by using alternative behaviors. Indifference isn't helpful, unless that indifference helps you protect yourself when coping with a potentially painful situation.

44. All people have a fundamental need to matter. We believe there's no greater empowering idea than believing you matter. Furthermore, when you show you care in this way at home or at work, you're saying to other people that they matter to you. Communicating the idea that others matter and you care shows the opposite of indifference.

45. People act out caring by learning about others and their work.

46. People want to have and need to communicate an expectation of caring.

47. Make sure you model the expectations you really want.

FINAL THOUGHTS:
WE MUST MAKE A PLACE!

48. Leaders need to learn the strengths, workflow, needs, difficulties, and the parts of work most satisfying to their people.

49. Learning is more powerful than teaching because teaching is linear and learning is circular.

50. Leaders need to develop a workplace culture conducive to learning. A learning culture provides an environment in which the entire work team is open and honest; it's a space where people can learn from one another. Leaders can learn about the work and the interactions of the team as everyone performs the work together.

51. Instead of focusing on causing people to learn – which we can't do; that's more like teaching – provide good information, a place for learning, and support to help another person use the information in the learning process.

52. The place you make in the workplace forms a foundation to support the continual learning people need to reach the maturity they seek.

ENDNOTE

As we've contrasted and compared natural horse training with the Theory Y approach to supervision, we've found interesting overlapping tenets and themes. Two discoveries are of utmost importance to us. First, both natural horse training and total quality management (a fairly recent and powerful development in industry and government) developed at approximately the same time in history. We believe this is an example of *zeitgeist*.

Zeitgeist is a German word that indicates the spirit of the time. That is, at a particular period of time in history, a general trend of thought or feeling (the *zeitgeist*) occurs and is displayed in any number of different disciplines. For us, the parallel development of natural horse training and the Theory Y approach to supervision reflects the shared spirit of this time in history. Other disciplines, such as the discipline of family systems therapy, have developed and will develop in parallel with the theories we discuss at length in our book.

Second, as a discipline or approach develops, current thought leaders in that discipline build on understanding by standing on the shoulders of those who came before them. We referenced two present-day cowboys, Jay Brewer and Louis Wood, many times in this book. Each of them has told us they learned the basics of what they know and practice from the people who wrote the books we referenced in the preface.

In natural horse training, the hierarchy of understanding started perhaps with Tom and Bill Dorrance, or perhaps before that, with the Native Americans. Cowboys such as Ray Hunt learned from the Dorrance brothers and developed the understanding further. Then, cowboys such as Buck Brannaman learned from Ray Hunt and brought the collective understanding to about where it is today. Jay Brewer and Louis Wood learned from people such as Pat Parelli, Clinton Anderson, and Buck Brannaman (all of whom we reference in this book) and, as we move into the future, are practicing and learning even more. As we mentioned earlier, this linear descent is similar to that of a family tree. This tree starts with the Dorrance brothers and branches down to include the many cowboys practicing natural horse training today.

In total quality management, the respected, most knowledgeable people practicing a couple of decades ago were W. Edwards Deming, Joseph Juran, and Philip Crosby. But where did Deming and Juran, for example, learn what they knew? Walter Shewhart mentored both of them. Other leaders during Shewhart's time included Douglas McGregor (Theory X and Theory Y) and Armand Feigenbaum (total quality control). Shewhart, McGregor, and Feigenbaum stood on the shoulders of Frederick Taylor (the father of scientific management), Mary Parker Follett (the mother of scientific management), and Frank and Lillian Gilbreth (experts in motion study and human factors). Today Edgar Schein, Jay Forrester, Herbert Simon, and those who studied under them are leading supervision and management into the future. Even more people are currently building and evolving management, supervision, and leadership understanding based on what they've learned from these leaders.

Throughout the book we've shown *zeitgeist* at work by capitalizing on the connections between natural horse training and the Theory Y approach to supervision. For example, we discussed the supervision lesson from natural horse training: looking at what happened before what happened happened. That's a clever way of saying people should think about the consequences of their actions before deciding on any one action to take. You'll find those words in many places: you'll hear them from cowboys, see them in books about training horses, and find them in many management and leadership books, particularly those that focus on vision as central to leadership and planning as fundamental to management. If this idea is repeated by so many, it must be a profound method of dealing with horses, business, and people.

AUTHOR BIOS

HAROLD KURSTEDT

 Harold Kurstedt has 30 years experience teaching strategic thinking, management systems engineering, and relationship competence to practicing professionals. Recently retired as the Hal G. Prillaman Professor Emeritus of Industrial and Systems Engineering from Virginia Tech, he is an award-winning professor. Harold is a co-founder and managing member of Newport Group LLC, a leadership consulting and training firm that works with industry, government organizations, professional associations, and people. He served as National President of the American Society for Engineering Management in 2004. Trained in traditional leadership at the Virginia Military Institute, Harold now focuses on new approaches in leadership oriented toward human relationships in an information-based society.

TIM THAYNE

Tim Thayne has been a passionate speaker, writer, and pioneer in the field of Marriage and Family Therapy for the past 20 years. From his doctoral work at Virginia Tech to now, his use of "Solution-Focused Leadership" has been instrumental in smoothing transitions inside corporations, partnerships, and families. After founding successful adolescent wilderness and residential treatment programs, in 2004 Tim created Homeward Bound to lead the movement to educate and support family's bringing their teens home following therapeutic treatment. Never one to underestimate the importance of transitions, Tim's strength lies in guiding business leaders and parents in their crucial roles as culture builders and change agents. His book *Home Again* details the process.

INDEX

A

abstractions
149-150

accountable, accountability
143, 208, 303, 314-315, 318,
318-319

affirmation, affirmed, affirm
29, 35, 52-53, 60, 91, 99,
103, 112-114, 116, 120, 123,
125, 150, 165, 185, 306, 315,
318-319

Anderson, Clinton
26, 104, 148, 166, 168, 213,
334

anxiety
44, 116, 186, 234, 264,
269-273, 280, 286, 327

appreciation, appreciate
19, 74, 86, 91, 100, 112-114,
116-117, 125, 129, 167, 252,
318

appropriate eye contact
70, 288

ask, asking
52, 55, 74, 78, 95, 102-103,
106-107, 110, 114, 124, 143,
150, 156, 164, 180-188, 208,
210-211, 220, 246, 249, 252,
266, 277, 279, 289, 298, 302,
305, 313, 318

attention to detail
143, 200

authentic
208-211

B

balk, balking, balked
75, 146, 162, 228

barn sour
131, 133, 141

barrier
234, 242, 258-259

**Believe: A Horseman's
Journey**
26, 168

body language
68-71, 112, 115, 166, 172,
174, 209, 232, 242-243, 277,
296-297, 305, 308, 324, 331

boundaries
135, 137, 142, 145-146, 148,
150-154, 167, 183, 217

Bowen, Murray
241

Brannaman, Buck
26, 62-63, 163, 168, 185, 203,
334

breaking horses
78, 311-312

Brewer, Jay
26, 55-56, 60, 69, 90, 103,
106-107, 146-147, 172, 184,
242, 269, 302, 314, 334

C

care, caring
21, 116, 143, 165, 168, 204,
234, 239, 246, 302-309, 315,
319, 331

carrot-and-stick approach
90, 186

change, changing
21, 25, 35-36, 44, 48, 54, 68,
73, 84, 89, 112-114, 117,
123, 139, 143, 153, 161-165,
179-184, 186-188, 192-193,
218-221, 225, 231, 238, 247,
249, 258, 272, 277, 285, 291,
294, 307, 320, 323-324, 338

character
60, 64, 113, 118, 131,
135-136, 276-280, 318, 328

circular
186, 312, 314, 316, 332

clarity
140, 142-143, 154, 181, 207,
213-216, 222, 320

*Clinton Anderson's
Lessons Well Learned*
26, 104, 148, 166

closed heart, closed hearted
227-230, 233-234, 238, 259,
267

coach, coaching
29, 35, 209, 257, 312, 314

collaboration
80, 113, 123, 164, 297

comfort
79, 81, 142-143, 163, 166-167,
180-181, 185, 194, 207-208,
211, 213-214, 216, 222, 235,
244, 270, 285, 324

**communication,
communicating, communicate**
26, 37, 61-62, 68, 70, 72,
73, 80-81, 86, 112, 114-116,
122-123, 142, 147-151,
153-155, 163, 166, 172, 174,
181-182, 184, 190, 192,
202-203, 209-210, 213-215,
221, 236, 261, 268, 289, 305,
307, 309, 312, 331

confidence
49, 55, 61-62, 87, 91, 106,
108, 112-113, 115, 118, 125,
135, 175, 194, 208, 212, 240,
263-264, 270, 277, 286-287,
289, 319, 326, 329

confront, confrontation
255, 291, 310

conscious
100, 139, 149, 256, 276,
295-296

contagious
44, 225, 243-245, 279, 305,
324

contribute, contribution
30, 54, 56, 61-62, 65, 69,
79-80, 85, 97, 108, 116, 118,
120, 123, 156-157, 174-175,
212, 236, 244, 247, 257,
263-265, 287, 294-295, 299,
307, 309, 321, 324, 326, 330

control
30, 43, 46-47, 52-54, 60,
75-77, 79-81, 119, 122,
132-134, 139-141, 172-174,
176, 188, 190, 195, 208, 219,
284-285, 329

Copenhagen interpretation
102, 104

covenant, covenantal
238-239

Covey, Stephen
84, 102, 104, 211

Cowboy Logic
26, 61, 73, 79, 86, 176, 180,
199, 216, 313, 316

creative, creativity
21, 36, 87, 95, 114, 174, 194,
208, 235-236, 280, 293-295,
299, 321, 330

Crosby, Philip
151, 334

culture
29, 70, 119, 153, 181, 239,
279, 314-315, 332, 338

D

decision making
47, 53, 65, 68, 119, 156, 186,
220, 260, 270, 320

Deming, W. Edwards
90, 95-96, 182, 245, 270, 334

direct report
56-57, 194, 204, 238, 245,
285, 312

discontinuity of organization
200-201

Dorrance, Bill
26, 88, 203, 266, 289, 334

Dorrance, Tom
26, 63, 203-204, 289, 334

draft horse
93-94, 96, 97

E

empower, empowerment
69, 115, 174, 176, 235, 240,
314-315, 318, 323

encourage, encouragement
29, 35, 48, 50-53, 56, 60, 62,
69, 73, 77, 80, 87, 89, 91,
99, 106, 109-118, 120, 122,
125-126, 143, 161, 164-165,
174, 185, 193, 207-209,
216-218, 228, 249, 257,
284-285, 297, 300, 303, 306,
312, 315, 319-320

enduring relationship(s)
81, 94, 235, 312, 317-319

exceptional moment(s)
55, 167, 231-232, 247-250,
305, 320, 324

expectation(s), expect
28, 34, 36, 46, 52, 68, 78-80,
83, 91, 104-105, 111, 118,
122-123, 129, 131, 136-137,
139-140, 142-143, 145-154,
159, 167, 169, 174, 176,
180-183, 189-190, 194, 199,
207, 209-217, 220, 222, 232,
236, 239, 258, 265-266, 268,
279, 286, 288, 298, 308, 310,
319-321, 326, 331

F

fail, failure
46, 61, 63, 94, 105-107, 116,
124, 187-188, 209-210, 213,
215, 238, 268, 316, 323

faith
45-47, 49, 117-118, 230,
260-261, 280

fear
43, 44, 77-78, 81, 87-88,
106, 113-114, 116, 122, 141,
168, 172, 174-176, 187, 234,
257, 264, 267, 269-272, 286,
290-292, 298, 312-313, 327,
329

fight
75-76, 80, 131, 133, 141, 257,
290

fit
153

flight
106, 257, 290

focus, focused
26, 30, 33-34, 42, 48-50,
53-54, 56-57, 60, 62-63, 71,
76, 80, 86-87, 94, 99, 100-105,
107, 109-110, 113, 115, 117,
119, 123-124, 137, 140, 148,
162, 174, 176, 179, 183,
193, 200-201, 208, 211, 216,
235, 240, 246-252, 257, 270,
284-285, 296-298, 304-305,
320, 324-325, 329, 335

H

HTEP
214-215

HTGT
201, 214-215

half-empty
247-248

half-full
247-249, 324

harmonious, harmony
26, 94, 171, 190, 243-244,
251-252, 263, 266-268, 281,
294, 326, 330

harness(es)
35, 47, 50, 52, 93-97, 120, 124

'head down, butt up, scratch dirt'
186, 220

heart
19, 36, 44, 56, 89, 94-96, 124, 131, 174, 213, 225, 227-235, 237-239, 245-246, 250, 256, 258-259, 267, 291, 302, 304, 323

Heisenberg's Uncertainty Principle
102, 104

homing strength
48, 60, 95

horse-focused
72

horse sense
28, 54, 62, 69, 73, 77, 90, 96, 106, 114, 148, 156, 168, 173, 184, 191, 204, 215, 242, 250, 259, 269, 278, 281, 289, 291, 297, 304, 313

Horse Sense for People
26, 72, 312

horse whisperer
62

Hunt, Ray
26, 60, 63, 73, 79, 86, 168, 171, 176, 180, 190, 199, 203, 216, 243-244, 250-253, 266, 268, 281, 313, 316, 334

I

imagination
80, 100, 143, 155-156, 159, 199, 218

indifference
164-165, 233-234, 280, 302, 304-310, 331

influence
64, 80, 84, 102, 104, 110, 117, 125, 143, 151, 161, 185, 241-244, 266, 276-278, 282, 301, 303, 307, 323-324, 328, 331

instinct(s)
47-48, 55, 133, 156, 172-173, 234, 257, 267, 289-290, 293, 302

integrity
60, 64, 208-210, 245

interdependence
213

J

judging role
74

Juran, Joseph
149, 334

K

kiss, kissing
184-185

L

leadership (leader)
46-47, 49, 51-53, 55-56,
59-65, 68-69, 73-74, 76-81,
83-90, 94, 96-97, 100-107,
109-110, 113-116, 119-124,
129, 133-135, 146-149, 164,
166-167, 175, 180, 185, 190,
192, 194, 201-204, 208,
213-215, 217, 221, 235,
238-241, 244-245, 248-253,
258, 260-269, 271, 279, 284,
286, 290-291, 294-296, 303,
308-309, 313-316, 320-321,
324-330, 332-335

lean forward
70, 288

learn, learning
25, 27, 33, 63, 67-69, 73-74,
79-80, 88, 90, 94, 96, 102,
104, 115, 121, 135, 137,
139-141, 146, 150, 154, 159,
163-168, 172, 174, 175, 180,
182, 186, 188, 199, 202-204,
211-213, 228, 231, 234, 236,
240, 243-244, 246, 248-249,
264, 266, 269, 273, 275-276,
299, 303-304, 305, 307-308,
312-321, 328, 331-332, 334

Lewin, Kurt
188

limbic system
186, 284

linear
312, 332, 334

listening, listen
26, 49, 67, 68-74, 78, 80, 87,
114-115, 121, 141, 143, 154,
163, 166, 184, 186, 202-204,
209, 213, 243, 288, 307,
312-313, 320, 324

looping
314, 316

love
19, 63, 129, 135, 194, 227,
233, 235, 238-240, 242, 280,
291, 302-304, 309, 316,
319-320, 323

M

management (manager)
25-30, 34, 68, 87, 90, 96, 101,
119, 121, 142-143, 149, 153,
171-176, 180, 182, 184, 188,
190, 192, 194, 199-201, 203,
219, 235, 238, 245, 251, 260,
279, 284, 286, 318, 320-321,
324, 326, 329, 333-335

management tools
28, 153

matter (you matter)
116, 126, 307, 310, 331

McGregor, Douglas
27, 334

method(s)
27, 63, 78-79, 96, 113,
172-173, 175, 181-184, 190,
211, 221, 244, 272, 294, 312,
315, 335

micromanagement
200

motivation
46, 79, 89-90, 113, 186, 265,
286-287, 316, 329

**mutual vision,
mutually-accepted**
29, 46, 52-53, 76, 119-120

N

natural homing sense
45, 48, 55

Natural Horse*Man*Ship
26, 101, 290, 316

natural horse trainer
26, 55, 62, 64, 77-80, 103,
106, 146, 164, 171-172, 175,
183, 185, 191, 203, 243, 289,
302, 321, 333-335

natural horse training
26-27, 30, 172, 175-176, 183,
311-312, 321, 333-335

'nits, gnats and tanks'
200-202, 221

O

old-school training/methods
172, 175, 321

open
70, 191, 288, 313

optimism
112, 137, 208, 243, 245, 270,
319, 326

oral communication
68

other-focused
19, 60, 62-63, 72, 74, 76, 80,
120, 235, 239-240, 246, 249,
281, 297, 299, 306, 319, 321,
328

P

Parelli, Pat
26, 101, 118, 230, 290-291,
316, 334

partnership, partner
27-28, 30, 33, 37, 77, 81,
95, 129, 134, 136, 141-142,
147, 156, 172, 174, 190, 194,
230, 265-267, 285, 290-291,
293-294, 303, 308, 317-318,
338

performance
65, 77, 113-114, 122, 174, 245,
248, 268, 272, 286-287, 298,
325

personal mastery
64-65, 110, 121, 245, 324

**phases of emergency
management**
101

power
68, 74, 80-81, 84, 94, 101,
121, 166, 209, 213, 235, 243,
279-280, 288, 320

pressure and release
161, 277, 285, 320

process
36, 49, 53, 71, 76, 78, 94,
99, 105, 108, 113, 122, 140,
143, 149, 153, 156, 176, 180,
189-195, 199, 201, 212, 215,
221, 231, 234, 269-270, 279,
297, 312, 314, 316, 320-321,
332, 338

produce, producer
89, 96, 153, 176-177, 244,
260-261

productive, productivity
30, 33, 77, 79-81, 88, 96-97,
114, 122-124, 147, 152, 176,
240, 260-261, 263, 265, 267,
273, 276, 288, 293, 294-296,
299, 321, 326, 327-328, 330

productive workplaces
263, 326

pushy and shovey
56

Pygmalion and Galatea effects
102, 105, 308

Q

Quality Is Free
151

R

receptive
70, 181

reflect
69-71, 83, 115, 123, 235, 244,
247-248, 252, 278, 375, 333

reflecting
29, 72, 213, 248, 307

reflection
70-72, 114-115, 121, 149,
186-187, 154, 209, 230, 320

refreezing
188

relationship(s)
25-28, 30, 34, 49, 56-57,
60, 62, 65, 68, 72-74, 78,
81, 84, 87, 94-96, 101, 113,
124, 133-134, 142, 171-172,
179, 187, 194, 205, 209-210,
213, 230, 234-235, 240, 242,
250-251, 257, 261, 263, 265,
267-268, 281, 288, 294-297,
301-303, 305, 307-309, 312,
317, 318-321, 323, 325-326,
328, 330

relaxed
65, 70, 163, 272, 277, 288, 299

release control
46-47

resources
29, 47, 52, 86-87, 113, 119,
123, 172, 181-183, 193-194,
199-200, 208, 220, 240, 252,
270, 314-315, 323

responsible, responsibility
53, 63, 80, 90, 107, 113,
150-151, 153-155, 158,
164-165, 173-174, 176, 183,
186, 189, 203, 212-214, 220,
235, 239, 245, 258, 269-270,
281, 287, 294, 313, 316, 321,
330

restraint(s)
94, 96, 124

requirements
149, 150, 151, 154, 239

Roberts, Monty
26, 72, 78, 175, 257, 311-312,
315

role model
208, 210, 245, 279, 310

round-pen
284-285

S

self-preservation
234, 284-286, 288-289, 302,
329

shirk, shirker
176-177, 260-261

'shower time'
294-295, 330

side pass
146-147

Sign Up
311

SOLAR
70, 288

solution, solutions
70, 131, 143, 153, 159-160,
162, 193, 208, 218

solution-focused leadership
30, 34-37, 49, 52-53, 55, 60,
77, 94, 102, 115-116, 120, 167

square(ly)
70, 103, 104, 288

starting horses
78, 312

Staub, Dusty
245

strategy, strategic
87, 154, 182-183, 215, 220,
271, 327, 337

strength(s)
28-30, 35, 39, 44, 46-57,
60-61, 63-64, 68, 74, 76-77,
80, 84-88, 94-97, 99-100,
102, 104-115, 140-141, 156,
174, 182, 185, 204, 208, 212,
215, 228, 235, 240, 248-252,
268, 292, 306, 308, 313-314,
318-321, 323, 332

subconscious
100, 149, 241, 256, 276, 295

success, successes, successful, succeed
27-28, 34-35, 37, 48, 54-55,
60-61, 63-65, 80-81, 87-88,
90, 95-97, 99-101, 103, 105,
107-108, 113, 115-116, 118,
120, 122, 125-126, 134, 139,
141, 143, 146, 148, 150-151,
154, 161-162, 166, 174, 185,
190-191, 194, 205, 207-208,
213-216, 248-249, 251-252,
267-270, 279-280, 292, 311,
316, 319-320, 324-325, 327,
338

SUD
272

supervision (supervisor)
25-30, 33-35, 37, 46, 63, 68,
75-77, 84, 87-89, 95-96, 119,
122, 142, 146-147, 152, 168,
172-176, 180-183, 185-188,
190-194, 199-201, 204, 208,
211-215, 217, 219-221, 238,
243-245, 250, 252, 257,
260-261, 264, 266-269, 273,
279, 285-287, 297, 303,
314-315, 318, 320-321, 324,
333-335

supply closet
260-261

surrender
47, 51-53, 77, 120, 122, 140,
320

support(s)
48, 50, 64-65, 86-87, 93-97,
106, 113, 118, 124-125,
162, 173, 181-182, 202-204,
213, 219, 235, 238, 248,
261, 264-265, 279, 287-288,
308-309, 315-316, 324, 332

systems engineers
191

T

tactical
182-183, 220

teach
27, 73, 108, 133, 136, 175,
180, 188, 203, 226, 251,
266, 272, 275-276, 278-279,
309-310, 312-314, 316-317,
328

tell, telling
19, 48, 55, 78, 116, 118, 150,
154, 184-186, 194, 201, 210,
220, 242, 246, 249, 265, 295,
299, 307, 317

The 7 Habits of Highly Effective People
211

The Faraway Horses
26, 62, 163

The Heart of Leadership
245

The Horse Whisperer
26, 62

The Man Who Listens to Horses
26, 78, 257, 312

The Power for True Success: How to Build Character in Your Life
279-280

Theory X
30, 77, 172-176, 219, 260,
286, 321, 334

Theory Y
27, 30, 75, 77, 143, 172-176,
219, 260, 321, 333-335

Think Harmony with Horses
26, 171, 190, 243, 251-252,
266, 281

token, tokens
245, 249

Torgersen, Paul
286

*True Horsemanship
Through Feel*
26, 88, 266

*True Unity: Willing
Communication between
Horse and Human*
26, 203, 289

trust, trusting
30, 34, 44-47, 49, 52, 56,
60-61, 65, 74, 77-78, 81,
95-96, 106-107, 111-112,
116, 118, 120, 122, 134, 143,
164, 166, 174, 176, 201-202,
205, 208, 214, 218, 221, 227,
230, 232, 235, 242, 246, 257,
263-264, 270-271, 278, 284,
286, 291, 302, 309, 312,
317-319, 329

U

understand, understanding
25, 27, 33, 37, 46-50, 52-53,
55, 61-62, 64, 72-76, 78-81,
84, 86-89, 101-102, 104,
122-123, 135, 137, 139, 142,
146-147, 151, 153, 154, 156,
167, 169, 172, 174-176,
180-183, 185, 191-193, 199,
201, 209, 211, 213, 235, 239,
244-245, 252, 255, 257-259,
264, 266-267, 277, 281, 289,
295, 309, 316-318, 320-321,
324, 333-335

unfreezing
188

unintended consequences
137-138, 143, 155, 157-160,
217-218, 320

unique, uniquely, uniqueness
48-49, 83-84, 87, 89, 123, 156,
165, 182, 193, 235, 240, 244,
265, 299, 323

urgency
130, 164, 166

V

Virginia Tech
33-34, 36, 286, 337-338

vision, shared vision
29, 35, 46, 49, 50, 52-53,
60-63, 65, 74, 76, 79, 81,
86-87, 95, 100-103, 119-121,
123-124, 135, 148, 155-156,
174, 182-183, 187, 201-202,
204, 208, 211-212, 215-216,
220, 252, 303, 306, 320, 335

W

WWA
214-215

WWWTB
201, 214-215

weakness
56, 100, 105-109, 125, 175,
280

Wood, Louis
26, 64, 79, 103, 164, 191, 203,
214, 244, 250, 296, 316, 334

work team
27, 50, 84, 88, 91, 110, 193,
250-251, 268, 287, 297, 303,
313-314, 330, 332

Y

Yates, John
238

Z

zeitgeist
333, 335

To order more books or to inquire about
Harold or Tim for speaking engagements
or workshops, please go to:

www.taking-the-reins.com

or

www.takingthereinsbook.com

CPSIA information can be obtained
at www.ICGtesting.com
Printed in the USA
FFOW02n1300060814
6702FF